The

BLACK

TRUTH

About History from Past to Present

ELOGEIA HADLEY

The Black Truth About History from Past to
Present, published and researched
by Elogeia Hadley, Author.

This publication is designed to provide accurate and
authentic information about the subject matter
covered. It is sold with the understanding that the
publisher does not provide legal, accounting, or
other professional services. If legal advice or other
expert assistance is required, the services of a
competent professional should be sought.

The cover and title page were designed
by Cynthia Everette with Ceverett Design, LLC

This book serves as a vital resource for education and historical awareness.
By purchasing it, you help fund necessary research and initiatives that deepen our understanding of the past.

CONTENTS

ACKNOWLEDGMENT

First, I would like to acknowledge the Most High God for the opportunity to share my knowledge. Knowledge is the key to life, helping us solve problems; without it, we would truly be lost. I want to acknowledge my mother and Father, Queen Isabella (Faye) and Prophet Lott (Julius), who taught me to investigate, seek knowledge, and always strive for the truth. As a child, my mother would tell me, "Use your head for more than just a hat rack," when I succumbed to peer pressure. I did not know what that meant at first. I was baffled by all her riddles and parables. But as I got older, I realized she was saying, "Use your head." She would always say this when I felt defeated:

"Anything man-made, you can master it; if a man can take his time and put it together, you can take the time to take it apart."

Then she would say, "You are an Aquarius, and they are some of the smartest people on the planet; you can find the answers. Just look deeper."

My mother was before her time. She understood the world, and she didn't like how black people seemed lost and didn't know who they were spiritually and intellectually. My parents understood that being black was beautiful. And with them, I learned to love all of myself.

I want to acknowledge all the master teachers, Historians, educators, scholars, anthropologists, and Egyptologists from the past to the present who have fought and worked tirelessly to give of themselves so that Black people can learn our true identities.

I want to acknowledge Anthony "Tony" Browder for his work, which has given me a deeper understanding. He was my awakening moment. Reading his book, "From the Browder File," was a source of enlightenment for me. It helped me look for more because I knew there was more to be found.

I want to acknowledge Tariq Nasheed for his documentary "Hidden Colors," which also brought light to my darkness, and all the master teachers he brought to my attention, from Dr. Joy Degruy, Dr. Frances Cress Welsing, Dick Gregory, Shahrazad Ali, Sabir Bey, Booker T. Coleman, Dr. Claude Anderson, Phil Valentine, and all others that participated in this excellent documentary.

I want to acknowledge my great-uncle Elishah, affectionately known as "Uncle Honey," who instilled in me a love for books as a child. Now and then, he would visit my Grandma Annie Bell's house, bringing the best pop-up books with smooth covers. I thought those books were magic. As time passed, it would be comforting for a lonely child. I could escape and use my imagination the way children used to. Thank you to all those ancestors who paved the way, making the path more tolerable; I will always be grateful and humble.

PREFACE

In this book, you will find information that you may not have encountered before and things our schools or parents may not have taught us about Black history.

This book is only a snapshot of many of the accomplishments and contributions of African people throughout the diaspora. It is not intended to offend anyone but to teach and give a glimpse of African contributions throughout the diaspora.

INTRODUCTION

I wrote this book after learning some history that I had not been taught in school or by my parents. I grew up in Chicago and was educated in the Chicago public school system in the 70s and 80s. Like many other educational systems, Chicago public schools taught a limited amount of Black history, and the majority favored white European conquests and accomplishments; some of it was true, some were fabrications, some were embellishments, and some were half-truths that left out vital facts.

For example, we were taught that Christopher Columbus discovered America when, in fact, he did not. Another example is how textbooks would separate the continent of Africa from Egypt when it is part of a continent. African history was non-existent before slavery, and educators would never mention African accomplishments and contributions in the history books.

While researching this book, my biggest challenge was *finding* Black/African history. The writers of history books purposely leave out African contributions, as if Africans didn't exist on their continent before the arrival of Europeans. The history books dismiss African contributions or code

Indigenous peoples as "occupants." They would even say it's a "mystery."

Many black people battle with feeling out of place, not having a culture, or not understanding that we played a huge part in world history. We see it all the time in school at culture fairs: the black children stand around with empty looks on their faces because we don't have culture, a craft, or a food that we can call our own. Or so we thought.

What is culture, anyway? Your culture is whatever you and your community do daily, including traditions and value systems. Black people have their share of traditions passed down from our ancestors and the traditions we picked up along the way.

Most black folks were taught that they had no part in history, and if they did, they were slaves or monkeys swinging from the trees in the African jungle. I was only taught bits and pieces about my history as a black person and almost nothing about being a black woman in ancient times or before slavery. We were taught Martin had a dream, Rosa sat down, oh, and "we were nothing but slaves" in the first place.

One day, I decided to help my then-11-year-old daughter with her culture fair at school. At this fair, the requirement was to represent your culture. So, being an American-born African descendant, I chose "America" and added "African American contributions." I collected information about our inventions for the culture fair, created a slideshow, and purchased an RBG (red, black, and green) flag and an American flag. We presented our food with American apple pie and sweet potato pie, both of which are cultural favorites among Black people in America.

I had my goddaughter sing the black national anthem, "Lift Every Voice and Sing," by J. Rosamond Johnson and James Weldon Johnson. For our craft, we provided beads for the children to make bracelets, and we also made Christmas cards because it was that time of year.

During the culture fair, I watched the visitors' facial expressions and overheard conversations of people shocked at what they saw because they did not know of these inventions. I saw pride in the faces of the black parents to see our accomplishments. At the end of the fair, we were told our display was the favorite of the evening, and many people were talking about it. There was also a point when I was homeschooling my youngest son due to issues at school, and when I got to the history part of teaching, I wanted to teach him some of his history. It was difficult because the information was spread out, coded in words, and buried or labeled as "mystery," or they would say "occupants." They would not mention the Africans as if Africa only existed 2000 years ago. So, I should pull all this information together to make it a little easier to find. Black people in America are owed at least the truth about our past, because where would the world be without African contributions?

This history is everyone's history, and if you are born in America or anywhere in the world, you should know that black people, the descendants of Africans, were more than just slaves. They were the descendants of kings, queens, warriors, masons, farmers, scientists, healers, architects, and so much more. Africans are the blueprint and the mother and father of the planet, so African history is world history.

CHAPTER 1

AT THE BEGINNING

Africa is recognized as the cradle of civilization and the birthplace of humanity. It is in regions like the Nile Valley that early humans emerged and where significant advancements in agriculture, architecture, writing, and governance took place. Civilizations such as Ancient Egypt, Nubia, and the Kingdom of Kush laid the foundation for modern science, mathematics, and spiritual systems. Africa's contributions to history continue to influence the world today, highlighting the continent's deep-rooted impact on civilization.

Cradle of Civilization

Some images in this book were created by Canva AI, Craiyon AI, and Pixabay powered by iStock.

Africa is humanity's birthplace, with unique fossil evidence tracing Homo sapiens and their ancestors through evolutionary stages. The Cradle of Civilization in South Africa has yielded crucial fossil remains of human predecessors. Modern humans emerged in Africa between 200,000-300,000 years ago, developing language around 50,000 years ago before beginning their migration out of Africa between 70,000-100,000 years ago.

The Eve Gene

Mitochondrial DNA (mtDNA) By analyzing mitochondrial DNA (mtDNA), passed from mother to child without recombination, scientists can trace back to the most recent common female ancestor, Mitochondrial Eve. This ancestral figure lived approximately 100,000 to 200,000 years ago, likely somewhere in Sub-Saharan Africa.

Many scientists believe the African woman is the only organism with Mitochondrial DNA with all the variations possible for every human being on Earth. It is called "Eve Gene." When a black woman's genetics mutates, she can create eye color, hair color, and skin pigmentation. The darkest African woman can make any human being on the planet. No other woman on Earth can do that. There was a time on this planet when all human life was in Africa, and it has been researched that all human life is a descendant of one woman. An African woman!

Dinkinesh "Lucy"
Dated to 3.2 million years

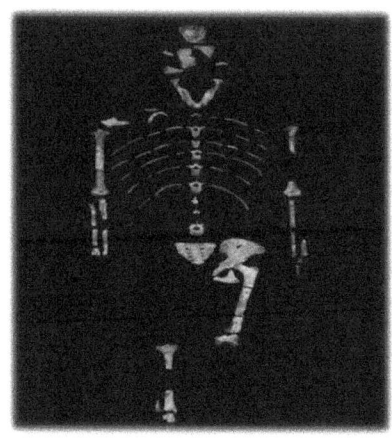 In 1974, near Hadar, Africa, in the Awash Valley, several hundred pieces of bone fossils made up about 40 percent of the skeleton of a female of the hominin species Australopithecus afarensis. The bones, labeled as AL 288-1, were named Dinkinesh by the Ethiopians, which means "you are marvelous," and Lucy by paleoanthropologist Donald Johansson of the Cleveland Museum of Natural History, Yves Coppens, and Maurice Taïeb. The Lucy specimen is an early australopithecine dated 3.2 million years ago.
Institute of Human Origins.
https://iho.asu.edu/about/lucys-story

4

Luzia "The Woman" of South America
Dated 12,000 years

Most are taught that African people first arrived in the Americas during the trans-Atlantic slave trade. However, that history is being changed as archaeologists continue to find evidence that Black Africans occupied the Americas before Mongolian Asians crossed the Bering Strait. According to the BBC documentary series Ancient Voices, the first people were the Black aboriginals of Africa or Australia. It is believed, from the evidence found, that invading Asians later may have entered married or massacred them. From all evidence, African descendants were the first to populate the land we called the Americas. Human skulls uncovered in

Lagoa Santa, Minas Gerais, Brazil, and South America were dated over 12,000 years old. In 1998, Walter Neves, an archaeologist from the University of Manchester, England, did measurements and reconstruction of the oldest skull called Luzia, and the measurements showed that Luzia was not mongoloid at all. Still, he determined the features were of a Negroid. So, Luzia was an African descendent. A black woman!

CHAPTER 2

INVENTIONS and CONTRIBUTIONS

Since the beginning, African people have contributed to history and the world, including inventions and other significant contributions.

OLDOWAN TOOLKIT
2.6 million years

The earliest clear evidence of stone tools comes from a 2.6-million-year-old site in Ethiopia. An early human ancestor called Homo habilis likely made them. These tools are known as the Oldowan toolkit and include choppers with one refined edge. Hammerstones are some of the earliest and simplest stone tools used to chip other stones into sharp-edged flakes, break nuts, seeds, and bones, and grind clay into pigment. The oldest stone tools, known as the

Oldowan toolkit consists of at least:

- Hammerstones that show battering on their surfaces.

- Stone cores that show a series of flake scars along one or more edges.

- Sharp stone flakes struck from the cores and offer functional cutting edges, along with lots of debris from percussion flaking.

8

IMHOTEP
Multi-genius

"The one who comes in "Peace."
Imhotep was born in the 27th century BCE, in Memphis, Egypt).

- He was a vizier
- Egyptian architect
- astrologer, physician, and
- statesman (chief minister to Djoser who reigned from 2630–2611 BCE, the second king of Egypt's third dynasty
- God of medicine in Egypt and in Greece, where he was identified with the Greek god of medicine, Asclepius). I
- architect of the step pyramid built at the necropolis of Ṣaqqārah in Memphis. The oldest monument of hewn stone is still in existence; the pyramid consists of six steps and is 200 feet (61 meters) tall. As a god of medicine, Imhotep was beloved as a
- he was the curer of everyday problems who could "provide remedies for all diseases" and "give sons to the childless."

LEWIS LATIMER
Inventor, *Incandescent Electric Lighting*

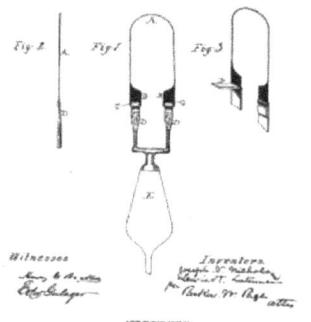

Latimer was one of the original draftsmen working for Thomas Edison. He was instrumental in helping to

- install the first electric plants in Philadelphia, New York City, and Montreal.
- He oversaw lighting installation in railroad stations and government buildings in Canada, New England, and London.
- He wrote the world's most thorough book on electric lighting, called "Incandescent Electric Lighting."
- In 1894, Latimer developed a safety elevator.
- He created locking racks for hats, coats, and umbrellas.

- He devised a device called the "Apparatus for Cooling and Disinfecting," which made railroad car toilets more sanitary and climate-controlled, leading to the development of air conditioning.
- He invented a way to encase a lightbulb's filament within a cardboard envelope, thereby providing a less expensive, more efficient bulb with a much longer lifespan.
- These improvements led to the adoption of electric lighting in homes and in streetlights.
- He painted portraits and wrote poetry and music.

GRANVILLE T. WOODS
Inventor: Telephone, Telegraph, Electrical Equipment, and Railroad Improvements

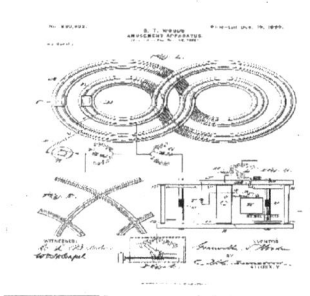

Woods was a manufacturer of telephones, telegraphs, and electrical equipment. He formed the Woods Railway Telegraph Company in 1884. He was also an inventor who patented a device that was part telephone and part telegraph, the "Telegraphony," in 1885.

He improved the steam boiler furnace and a telephone transmitter with superior range and clarity for long-distance communications. He also invented the

- Synchronous Multiplex Railway Telegraph or "induction telegraph" allowed messages to be relayed from moving trains to railway stations. Dispatchers could now know the location of a train, which improved safety and decreased railway accidents.

- Woods held over 25 U.S. patents for various electrical, mechanical, and telegraph inventions.
- including an electric railway and a
- an electric roller coaster called Figure Eight.

Granville Woods' inventions were often imitated by others, including Thomas Edison. After Woods defeated Edison in court for the second time, Edison decided it was futile to keep fighting Woods and offered him a position with the Edison Company.

ELIJAH MCCOY
Inventor, *Engineer, "The Real McCoy"*

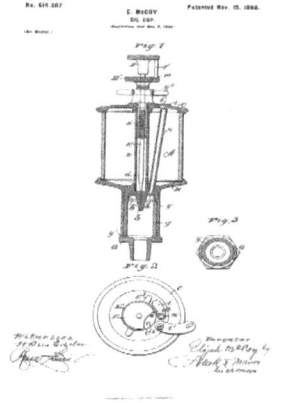

McCoy was a Canadian-born inventor and engineer of African American descent who held 57 U.S. patents, many related to the lubrication of steam engines. He also started The Elijah McCoy Manufacturing Company in 1920. Inventions included:

- Oil dripping cup.
- Ironing the table, after his wife expressed a need.
- Sprinkler system for lawn watering

GEORGE WASHINGTON CARVER
Scientist, Inventor, and Agriculturist

The United States Army utilized Carver's products during World War I. Henry Ford, head of Ford Motor Company, invited Carver to his Dearborn, MI, plant, where the two devised a way to use goldenrod, a weed, to create synthetic rubber. He was elected a Fellow of the Royal Society of Arts, Manufactures and Commerce of Britain. In 1916, he was awarded the Theodore Roosevelt Medal for Distinguished Research in Agricultural Chemistry. Carver:

- Taught methods for improving the soil.
- Instructed farmers to plant peanuts, which could be harvested quickly and fed to livestock.
- Produced more than 300 products that could be developed from the lowly peanut, including ink, facial cream, shampoo, and soap.
- Developed over 115 products derived from sweet potatoes, including flour starch and synthetic rubber.
- Developed over 75 products from the pecan.

- Created dozens of uses for discarded corn stalks.
- Created dyes and paints from clay.
- Co-authored papers on preventing and curing fungus diseases affecting cherry plants.

SARAH BOONE
Inventor, a collapsible ironing board

 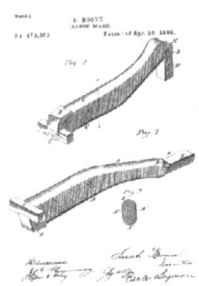

Boone was among the first African American women to receive a U.S. Patent. In 1892, she received a patent for

- a narrow, collapsible ironing board with a padded cover specifically designed for the fitted clothing worn during that era: this is the first version of a modern ironing board (before this, people used a plank of wood supported by two chairs).

W.H. RICHARSON
Inventor, back and front-facing baby bassinet.

Richardson improved the first baby carriage (invented by William Kent in 1733). These improvements made the buggy more manageable and safer.

He invented

- a bassinet that could face the front and back

and adjusted the axles on the wheels so that the carriage was nimbler in tight spaces.

Dr. PHILIP EMEAGWALIE
Computer scientist

Emeagwalie attended Oregon State University at 17 and obtained a BS in mathematics before earning three other degrees: a Ph.D. in Scientific computing from the University of Michigan and two master's degrees. He was fascinated by bees, and in 1989, after noticing the efficiency with which bees construct and work with honeycomb, Emeagwali emulated the bees' honeycomb construction using 65,000 processors to invent the world's fastest computer, which performed computations at 3.1 billion calculations per second.

Dr. JESSE ENRNEST WILKINS, JR.
Mathematician, shield Gamma Radiation

Wilkins was the University of Chicago's youngest student, at just 13. He earned his bachelor's and master's degrees in mechanical engineering from New York University. He taught mathematics at the Tuskegee Institute, and worked at the Metallurgical Laboratory at the University of Chicago, where he

- contributed to the "Manhattan Project." His greatest contribution was the development of mathematical models to explain gamma radiation. He worked on developing a shield against gamma radiation.

LISA GELOBTER
Web Animation and Communications

Gelobter is the founder/CEO of TEQuitable. She developed several Internet technologies, including-

- Shockwave Flash,
- Animated GIFs,
- Brightcove,
- Joost and The Feedroom.
- She was a member of senior management for the launch of Hulu,
- Chief Digital Service Officer for the United States Department of Education during the Obama administration, and
- the Former Black Entertainment Television Networks (BET) Vice President.

DR. SHIRLEY JACKSON
Theoretical Physicist and Inventor

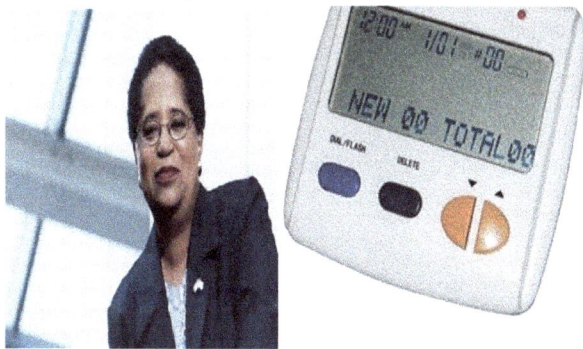

Jackson received a Bachelor's and Doctorate in physics from the Massachusetts Institute of Technology (MIT). She used her knowledge of physics to foster advances in telecommunications research while working at Bell Laboratories. Her inventions and contributions include:

- Portable fax
- Touch-tone telephone
- Solar cells
- Fiber optic cables
- The technology behind caller ID and call waiting

MARIE VAN BRITTAN BROWN AND ALBERT BROWN
Closed-circuit Television Security System

Marie Van Brittan Brown and her partner Albert Brown applied for a patent for a

- closed-circuit television security system, the forerunner to the modern home security system.
- Brown's system featured four peepholes and a camera that could slide up and down to look out each one, and the camera fed information to a monitor.
- Brown's system also included a feature where a person could unlock a door with a remote control. Her invention was the first in a long string of home-security inventions for homeowners and businesses.

Dr. BETTY W. HARRIS
Chemist, Explosives

Harris was a noted expert in the chemistry of explosives. She is a research chemist at the Los Alamos National Laboratory in New Mexico. She has worked in hazardous waste treatment and environmental restoration of facilities contaminated with propellants, gun propellants, and explosives. For her achievements, she has received the Governor's Trailblazer Award.

DR. PATRICIA BATH
Ophthalmologist and Inventor

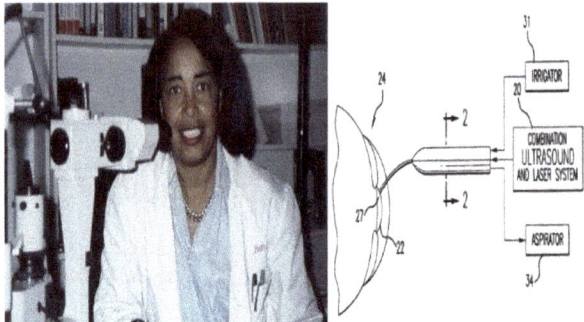

As a noted ophthalmologist and inventor, Dr. Bath has dedicated her life to treating and preventing visual impairment. In 1985, she developed.

- a specialized tool and procedure for the removal of cataracts. The Laserphaco Probe vaporizes the cataract and defective lens material, which is then removed by suction tubes. A replacement is then inserted using the Laserphaco Probe. The invention and procedure significantly increased the accuracy and results of cataract surgery.

- Dr. Bath has helped restore the sight of several people blinded by cataracts for up to 30 years.

Dr. HENRY SAMPSON
Mobile Communications, Gamma-Electric Cell

In 1971, Sampson co-invented
- the "Gamma-Electric cell" with George H. Miley. The Gamma-Electric cell produces stable high-voltage output and current to detect nuclear radiation in the ground. In 1973, Sampson invented an
- improvement to the propellant section of rocket chambers.

DR. MARK DEAN
Computing Inventor

Dr. Dean is one of the most prominent black inventors in computers. He holds a bachelor's degree in electrical engineering from the University of Tennessee, a master's degree in electrical engineering from Florida Atlantic University, and a Ph.D. in electrical engineering from Stanford. Since he began working at IBM in 1980, he has been instrumental in the invention of the

- Personal Computer (PC).
- He holds three of IBM's original nine PC patents and over 20 total patents.
- He helped IBM make changes in computing that increased computers' processing speed.
- His most recent computer inventions occurred while leading the team that produced the 1-Gigahertz chip, which contains one million transistors and has nearly limitless potential.

MADAME CJ WALKER
Inventor, Hair Care

Madame CJ Walker was born and raised in the South and had issues with her scalp just like most African American women. After working for

another black woman selling hair products, she developed her own, making her popular. Her products made her an entrepreneur and one of the first black female millionaires. Mrs. walker also had other ideas that made her stand out:

- opened a factory and a beauty school in Pittsburgh in 1908
- transferred the "Madame CJ Walker Manufacturing Company" operations to Indianapolis, where she manufactured cosmetics, including her "Wonderful Hair Grower."
- Trained sales beauticians using the "Walker Method."

- promoted her "cleanliness and loveliness" philosophy to advance African Americans' status.
- She organized clubs and conventions for her representatives, recognizing successful sales and philanthropic and educational efforts among African Americans.
- She traveled throughout Latin America and the Caribbean, promoting her business and recruiting others to teach her hair care methods.
- She donated the most significant amount of money by an African American toward constructing an Indianapolis YMCA in 1913.
- Her business was valued at more than $1 million.

MARJORIE STEWART-JOYNER
Inventor, Hair Care

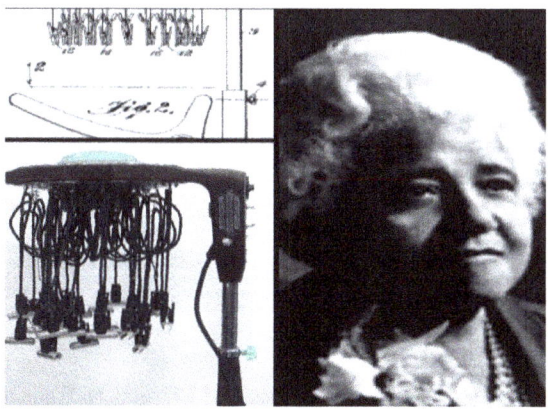

In 1928, Stewart-Joyner patented the "Permanent Waving Machine" that simplified straightening and curling hair. Along with educator Mary Bethune McLeod, Marjorie co-founded the United Beauty School Owners and Teachers Association and was active in fundraising for black colleges. She received a bachelor's degree in psychology from Bethune-Cookman College in 1973 at 77 years of age.

LYDA NEWMAN
Inventor, Hairbrush Improvements

Was an African American inventor, women's rights activist, and hairdresser by trade. While she was not the original inventor of the hairbrush, Newman's improvements contributed to the evolution of the modern hairbrush, especially for African hair

SARAH E. GOODE
Inventor, Folding Cabinet Bed

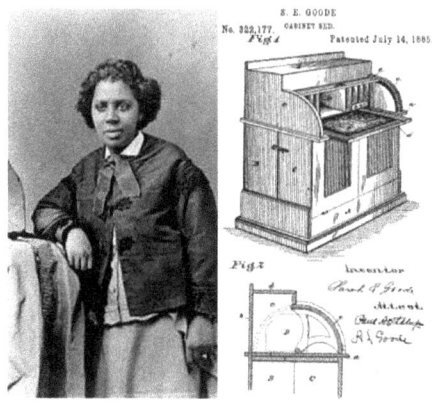

A Chicago-based inventor, business owner, and entrepreneur, Goode was the first African American woman to be granted a patent by the U.S. Patent and Trademark Office for a

- folding cabinet bed, which was the predecessor to the modern Murphy bed (1885).

ANNIE MALONE
Inventor, Cosmetics

In 1902, Malone developed and manufactured her line of hair care products called Poro Products for African American women. She inspired Madame C.J. Walker, a notable African American entrepreneur. In addition to selling her products door to door, Malone founded Poro College in 1917 in St. Louis, the first center in America dedicated to studying and teaching Black cosmetology.

GARRET MORGAN
Inventor, Businessman, Community Leader

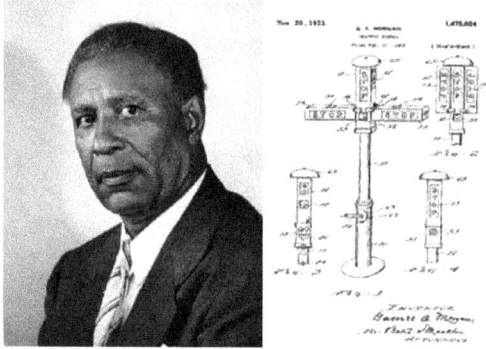

Although his education was limited to elementary school, Kentucky-born Morgan began his career as a sewing-machine mechanic.

- He made several notable improvements to the sewing machine,
- developed a chemical hair-straightening product,
- created a respiratory device that would later be used in World War I gas masks.
- invented a three-position traffic signal.
- He started a successful company based on his hair products.
- In 1908, Morgan co-founded the Cleveland Association for Colored Men, which later merged with the National Association for the Advancement of Colored People.

PHILLIP DOWNING
Mailbox Inventor

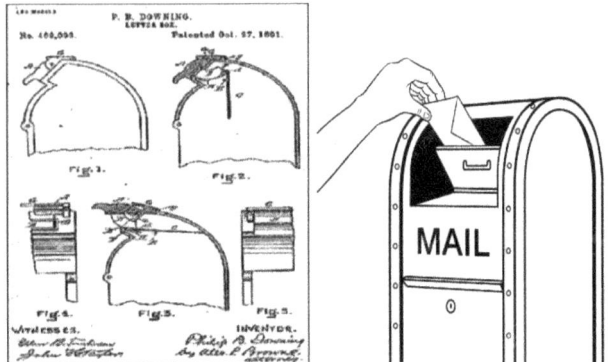

Downing invented the first street letter mailbox with a hinged door that could close and protect the mail. In 1891, he received two patents for the street letter box and a patent for a mechanical device for operating street railway switches.

THOMAS JENNINGS
Inventor, Dry Cleaning

 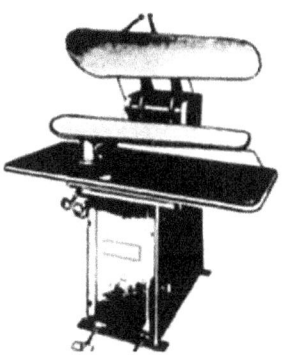

In his clothes cleaning business, Jennings was a tailor who experimented with cleaners that would remove stains without harming the fabric. He developed a process called.

- dry scouring, which was the forerunner of modern dry-cleaning. He received a U.S. patent for this invention in 1821: the first African American patent recipient.

THOMAS ELKINS
Inventor, Refrigeration

Elkins was an avid inventor whose focus was on improving everyday household items.
including

- a combination dining/ironing/quilting table (1870) and
- the chamber commode (1872).
- refrigerator in 1879, or as he put it, a refrigeration apparatus "for food or corpses." The device included a covered trough that was kept chilled through continuous circulation of chilled water or other fluid through metallic coils.

FREDERICK McKinley JONES
Inventor, Refrigeration

Jones held over 60 U.S. patents. Forty of those were in the field of refrigeration.
He invented it.

- automatic refrigeration systems for long haul trucks and
- railroad cars, a roof-mounted cooling system,
- refrigerators, and air conditioning units for military field hospitals.
- a self-starting gas engine,
- a ticket dispensing machine,
- two-cycle internal combustion engine.
- and made improvements to the movie projectors.

Jones was posthumously awarded the National Medal of Technology in 1991, the first black inventor to ever receive such an honor.

Dr. LONNIE JOHNSON
Inventor, Nuclear Engineer

Dr. Johnson, a rocket scientist and inventor,

- the Super Soaker Water Gun, a popular toy made from a used water bottle, plastic tubing, and duct tape.
- He founded start-up companies Excellatron Solid State and Johnson Electro-Mechanical Systems.
- Today, Johnson is developing thin film batteries for cell phones and aerospace applications.

Dr. PERCY JULIAN
Chemist, chemical synthesis

Dr. Julian was a pioneering research chemist known for his work in

- synthesizing plant-derived medicines, including hormone replacements.
- He later became a chemistry instructor at Fisk University and earned a Ph.D. from the University of Vienna in 1931, becoming one of the first African Americans to do so.
- The Calabar bean to treat glaucoma.
- In 1936, Julian extracted a soy protein used by the U.S. Navy to create Aero-Foam, a fire retardant crucial during World War II. He continued his contributions to hormone synthesis and
- Founded Julian Laboratories in 1953.

ALFRED L CRALLE
Inventor, Household Improvement

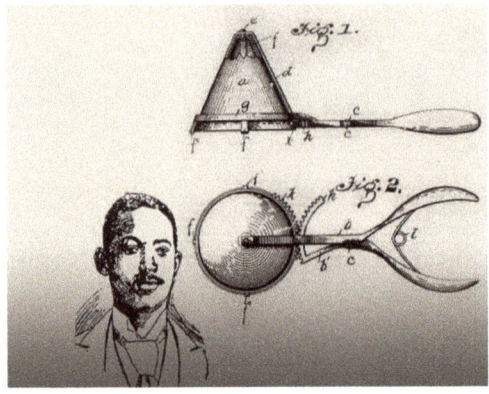

Cralle designed the ice cream scoop in 1897, a device that helped to keep ice cream and other soft foods from sticking to the scoop. It was initially called an Ice Cream Mold and dish. It was easy to operate with one hand, strong, durable, effective, and inexpensive. It could be constructed in almost any desired shape, such as a cone or a mound, with no delicate parts that could break or malfunction. Cralle was also a successful Pittsburgh business promoter.

TONY HANSBERRY II
Inventor, Medical Advancement

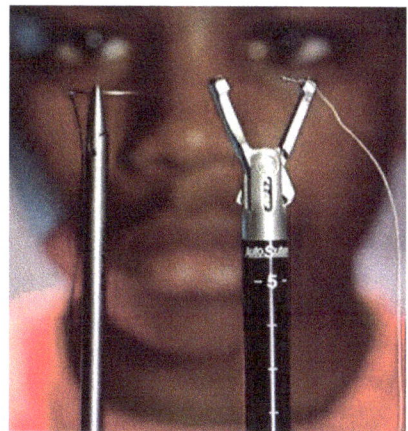

In 2010, at just 15 years old, Hansberry developed.

- a surgical stitching technique for hysterectomy patients, which decreased hospital stays and made for more efficient surgeries. At 18, Hansberry was dubbed "The next Charles Drew" (Dr. Drew pioneered the blood transfusion field and was the discoverer of the four blood types). Hansberry was honored at the McDonald's 365 Black Awards for his medical contributions. Today, Hansberry is a biomedical engineering student at Florida A&M University.

C.R. PATTERSON and F.D. PATTERSON
Inventors, Automobile Improvements

C.R. Patterson   F.D. Patterson

C.R. Patterson started as a carriage builder, building 28 different types of horse-drawn carriages. His son Frederick initiated the conversion from horse-drawn carriages to automobiles, and the Patterson-Greenfield company became the first African-American-owned automobile manufacturer.

- The first Patterson-Greenfield automobile debuted in 1915. It was comparable to its contemporary, the Ford Model T. 150 of the $850 vehicles were built.
- The company soon switched to manufacturing trucks, buses, and other utility vehicle bodies. Its bus bodies became popular as Midwestern school districts

converted from horse-drawn to internal-combustion-fired transportation by 1920.

RALPH GILLES

Inventor, Automobile Improvements

Ralph Gilles is an American Canadian automobile designer, the president and CEO of the SRT Brand, and the senior vice president of design at Chrysler Group LLC. His most notable contributions are the styling of the 2005 Chrysler 300 and the design team leader that created the 2014 SRT Viper.

JOHN ALBERT BURR
Inventor, Household Improvements

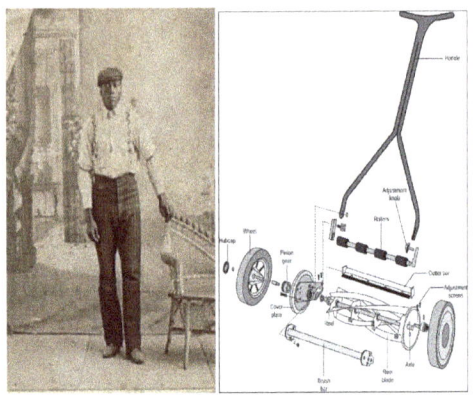

In 1899, Burr patented an improved rotary lawn A blade not easily plugged with lawn clippings allowed mowing close to buildings and wall edges. Burr continued to patent improvements to his design. He also designed devices for mulching clippings, sifting, and dispersing them. Today's mulching power mowers may be part of his legacy, returning nutrients to the turf rather than bagging them for compost or disposal. In this way, his inventions helped save labor and were suitable for the grass. He held over 30 U.S. patents for lawn care and agricultural innovations.

DR. JAMES WEST
coinventor, electric Microphone

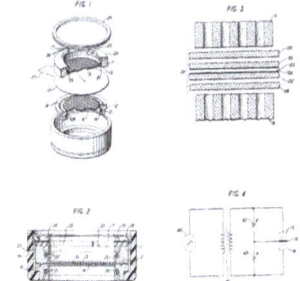

In 1960, Dr. James West and German physicist
Gerhard M. Sessler set out to create an
- affordable and compact microphone. At that
  time, most telephones used expensive
  condenser microphones that required large

batteries, making them impractical for home use.

- The electret microphone they developed solved these issues by being inexpensive, durable, and able to hold a charge without a power source. Completed on January 14, 1964, it received patent number 3,118,022 for their "electroacoustic transducer." By 1968, the microphone was mass-produced and quickly became the industry standard,
- influencing the design of microphones, tape recorders, camcorders, baby monitors, hearing aids, and modern telephones.

DR. HADIYA-NICOLE GREEN
Physicist, Inventor, cancer treatment

Dr. Hadiyah-Nicole Green

Dr. Green, a physicist with a Ph.D. from UAB, developed a laser-activated nanoparticle cancer treatment that bypasses chemotherapy and surgery. Motivated by personal loss, she received a $1.1 million grant for her research and aims to make cancer treatment accessible while mentoring Black students in science.

OTIS BOYKIN
Inventor, Medical Improvements

 Otis Boykin created everyday electronic devices, but he is best known for improving the pacemaker. In 1959, he received a patent for

- a wire precision resistor, later used in radios and televisions.
- He also created a device used by the U.S. military for guided missiles and by IBM for computers.

Dr. DANIEL HALE WILLIAMS
Surgeon, Inventor, Medical Improvements

Williams opened his medical practice in Chicago in

- 1883, when he earned a stellar reputation for professionalism and sterile medical procedures.
- He was appointed to the Illinois State Board in 1889 and created a multi-cultural hospital, the Provident Hospital and Training School Association, which was opened in 1891. Many of today's medical practices can be attributed to Williams' insistence on the highest standards concerning procedures and sanitary conditions.
- On July 9, 1893, Williams performed the first open heart surgery after repairing the heart of a man who had been stabbed multiple times; the patient lived, and Dr. Williams made history.

Dr. SAMUEL KOUNTZ
Surgeon, Kidney Transplant

Kountz was a renowned surgeon and pioneer in organ transplants.

- He was the first African American to receive an M.S. in biochemistry from the University of Arkansas in 1958.
- His Stanford University School of Medicine residency focused on surgery and kidney research.
- In 1961, Kountz discovered that monitoring blood flow into a new kidney and administering methylprednisolone to the patient after surgery allowed the body to accept the new organ.
- Kountz worked with Folker Belzer to create the Belzer Kidney Perfusion Machine, which kept kidneys alive for 50 hours after being removed from the donor.

- Thanks to Kountz's pioneering work, kidney transplants are routine today. Kountz also traveled the world to share his expertise.

ALEXANDER MILES
Automatic elevator doors

Alexander Miles was an African American inventor and businessman who invented automatic elevator doors, for which he received U.S. patent 371,207 on October 11, 1887. Before this innovation, riders had to manually close both the shaft and elevator doors, leading to dangerous accidents, including falls down the elevator shafts. Miles's daughter nearly fell into a shaft, so he created a safer solution. His patented mechanism for automatically opening and closing elevator shaft doors significantly improved elevator safety and functionality.

ALICE H. PARKER
Gas furnace

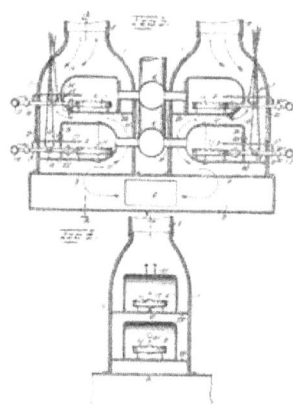

Alice H. Parker was an influential African American inventor known for her 1919 patent for a natural gas central heating system. This design drew cool air into a furnace, heated it, and circulated warm air through ducts, revolutionizing home heating.

Born in 1895 in Morristown, New Jersey, Parker graduated from Howard University Academy. Her invention improved traditional fireplaces, increasing safety and reducing the need for wood.

Despite the racial and gender barriers of her time, Parker's groundbreaking work laid the foundation for modern heating systems and showed how one visionary can transform everyday technology.

Vivien Thomas
Chemist, "blue baby"

Vivien Thomas was an African American medical
pioneer who made significant contributions to
cardiac surgery despite facing racial barriers. After
losing his medical school savings during the Great
Depression, he became a laboratory assistant to Dr.
Alfred Blalock at Vanderbilt University and later
joined him at Johns Hopkins.
Thomas developed life-saving procedures for "blue
babies" with congenital heart defects, guiding
surgeries and training surgeons while working as a
bartender. Although initially unrecognized, he
received an honorary doctorate from Johns Hopkins
in 1976 and served as instructor emeritus of
surgery. He passed away in Baltimore at 75, leaving
a legacy in the field.

DR. CHARLES RICHARD DREW
Surgeon, inventor of blood transfusion

He was an African American physician and surgeon known for his work in blood transfusion. Drew graduated from Amherst College in 1926, McGill University in 1933, and Columbia University in 1940. He researched blood plasma preservation and developed methods for processing and storing it in "blood banks." During World War II, he organized blood plasma programs for the U.S. and Great Britain and fought against the exclusion of African American blood from plasma supplies. Drew resigned in 1942 after the military mandated that African American blood be stored separately. He then served as a surgeon and professor at Freedmen's Hospital and Howard University until his fatal car accident in 1950.

ONESIMUS
Inventor, known as the father of vaccines.

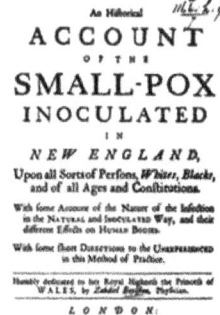

In the early 1700s, Onesimus, an enslaved African man (likely Akan), shared with Cotton Mather his enslaver, a Puritan clergyman the practice of smallpox inoculation that was common in his homeland in Africa. During Boston's 1721 smallpox outbreak, this knowledge proved invaluable - Onesimus's introduction of variolation helped control the epidemic and influenced early American public health practices.

NATHAN GREEN
Inventor, Jack Daniel's Whiskey, Master Distiller
And Uncle Nearest's whiskey

Nathan "Nearest" Green was a blackhead stiller, or
master distiller, who was born into slavery and
emancipated after the Civil War. He became the
first African American master distiller in the United
States and taught distilling techniques to Jack
Daniel, founder of the Jack Daniel's Tennessee
Whiskey distillery. Though he played a crucial role
in training Jack Daniel, Green didn't receive proper
recognition during his lifetime. To honor his legacy,
author Fawn Weaver founded the Nearest Green
Foundation, which creates a museum and
scholarships for Green's descendants. Today, Uncle
Nearest whiskey is produced and available for
purchase.

GEORGE CRUM
Inventor, Food Improvement

George Crum, a chef, accidentally invented the potato chip in 1853. To teach a picky customer a lesson, he sliced a new batch of potatoes as thinly as he could and then fried them until they were hard and crispy. The dish was a hit, and soon Crum opened his own restaurant that featured a basket of potato chips on every table. Crum never patented his invention, which is now ubiquitous with snacking.

JAMES HEMINGS
MAC n CHEESE

James Hemings a chef, and enslaved man by Thomas Jefferson, is credited with creating mac and cheese. While Jefferson often gets credit for popularizing it in the United States, Hemings learned to cook it and introduced one of America's favorite foods.

RICHARD FLEMMING JR.
Inventor Guitar

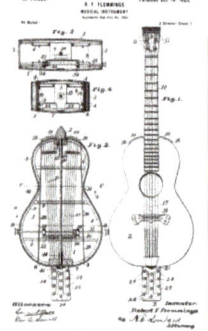 

Flemming is best known for inventing the guitar
that was out of boredom with the same musical
sounds at the time. Flemming Jr. developed the
popular instrument on March 3, 1886. Other than
the fact that he was an African American male from
Mississippi, all other peripheral details about Robert
Flemming Jr.'s life are a mystery. Flemming
invented a guitar he called the "Euphonica" that he
believed would produce a louder and more resonant
sound than a traditional guitar. The U.S. Patent
Office granted Flemming a patent (no. 338,727) on
March 30, 1886. He also received a Canadian

ANNA MANGIN
Inventor, pastry fork

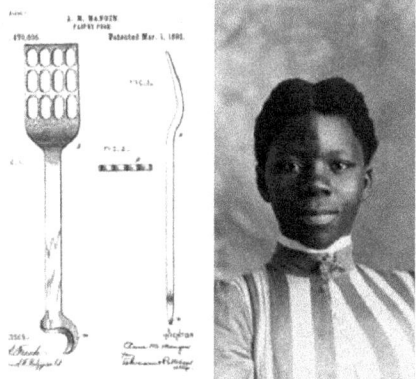

Mangin invented a pastry fork for mixing pastry dough. The utensil made it easy to mix dough for pie crusts, cookies, butter and flour pastries, and other baked goods without manipulating the ingredients physically. The fork is also used to beat eggs, mash potatoes, and prepare salad dressings. She received a patent for her invention in 1892.

Dr. ROY ALLELA
Inventor, sign IO glove

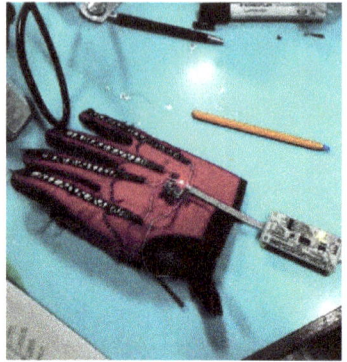

In 2017, 25-year-old Kenyan Roy Allela invented the Sign-IO gloves that translate signed hand movements to audible speech. The invention allows deaf people to "talk" even to those who don't understand sign language. The gloves, which are currently a prototype, are connected via Bluetooth to an Android app (which Allela also invented) that uses a text-to-speech function to convert the hand gestures to vocal speech.

MICHEAL JACKSON
entertainer, singer-songwriter, and inventor
Antigravity shoe

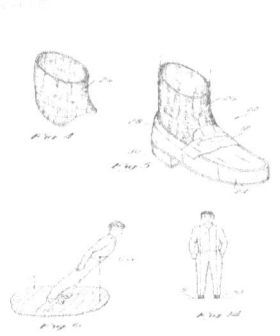

The most epic dance move in the world was not a result of Jackson's "gravity-defying" dancing skills in the video Smooth Criminal, Jackson fights in a nightclub, and in the dance battle, he leans 45 degrees without falling. Mr. Jackson invented an anti-gravity shoe, and the invention proved to be patentable and on October 26, 1993, the U.S. Patent and Trademark Office officially granted their request for patent rights over "Method and means for creating anti-gravity illusion," U.S. Patent No. 5,255,452.

BISHOP CURRY
Inventor, The Oasis

In 2017, at age 11, after a neighbor's baby died after being left alone in a hot car, Curry invented a device called the Oasis that would sense if a child were left alone in a car and send a text alert to the police. The device detects movement in the car, blows cool air on the baby, and automatically calls emergency responders. He prototyped the idea with his dad, who then pitched it to Toyota (his employer). Toyota recognized the boy's innovative efforts. The device is currently in development, and Curry hopes it will be on the market soon.

MIKE BELLOT
Inventor, Solo Bag

said Mike Bellot, the 26-year-old entrepreneur.
Earned a bachelor's degree in international political
economy (IPE) and a master's in international
Trade from the University of Tamkang in Taiwan,
Mike is the co-founder and CEO of Solobag in
Haiti. After the tragic loss of a family member,
Mike Bellot created the Solo Bag, an innovative
school backpack that provides light for reading,
studying, and charging mobile phones.
Shanique Yates Posted on February 25, 2021

CHAPTER 3

SCIENCE AND ASTRONOMY

Black people were not allowed to acquire formal education during slavery. Various laws were passed to keep blacks from any literacy in the wake of the slave rebellions and revolts. Nonetheless, countless black scientists have made significant contributions to society and humanity. Here are a few scientific contributions

KATHERINE JOHNSON, DOROTHY VAUGHN, MARY JACKSON
NASA, "The Human Computers"

Before modern computers, people like Johnson, Vaughn, Jackson (and others) were 2hired by the National Advisory Committee for Aeronautics (NACA) now known as NASA, to make wind tunnel measurements and calculations and form mathematical equations. They were immortalized in the movie "Hidden Figures."

Dr. Roger Arlinger Young
Scientist, Zoologist

Roger Arliner Young was a pioneering Black
woman in zoology who overcame significant
challenges. She initially studied music at Howard
University but switched to biology after a course
with Ernest Everett Just. Young became the first
Black woman to earn a Ph.D. in zoology and
conduct research at the Marine Biological
Laboratory.
Her research focused on paramecium and the effects
of radiation on sea urchin eggs. Despite facing
obstacles, she published several articles and worked
at various universities, earning her M.S. in 1926 and
her Ph.D. in 1940.

69

Young's journey included caring for her invalid mother and being dismissed from Howard University in 1936. She returned to lecture at Southern University until she died in 1964, demonstrating remarkable resilience.

DR. RONALD ERWIN McNAIR
NASA Astronaut and Physics

SOME IMAGES IN THIS BOOK WERE CREATED BY CANVA AI, CRAIYON AI, AND PIXABAY POWERED BY ISTOCK

Ronald McNair was an astronaut on the Space Shuttle Challenger, which tragically exploded shortly after takeoff in 1986, killing all crew members. An MIT-trained physicist, McNair operated the robotic arms that released satellites during the shuttle's missions. He logged 191 hours in space over 122 orbits before the disaster. Notably, he was also photographed playing his saxophone during his first mission. He was a 5th-degree black belt and AAU karate gold medalist.

CAPTAIN WINSTON E. SCOTT
NASA,
Navy Captain and NASA Astronaut

Winston Scott is a former Navy Captain and NASA astronaut with a degree in aeronautical engineering and avionics. After graduating from Florida State University, he entered Naval Aviation Officer Candidate School in December 1972. As a Naval Aviator, he logged hours in the F/A-18 Hornet and A-7 Corsair. Scott served as a mission specialist on STS-72, conducting two spacewalks, and was a crew member on the space shuttle Endeavour's nine-day flight in January 1996. He retired from NASA and the U.S. Navy in 1999 and is now a published author and advisor.

COLONEL FREDERICK DREW GREGORY NASA,

Astronaut, Administrator, and
The First Black Man to Command a Space Shuttle

SOME IMAGES IN THIS BOOK WERE CREATED BY CANVA AI, CRAIYON AI, AND PIXABAY POWERED BY ISTOCK

Gregory earned a Bachelor of Science degree from the United States Air Force Academy and a master's in information systems from George Washington University. He joined NASA and embarked on his first mission in 1977. In 1985, he became the first Black man to command a space shuttle during the Challenger mission, followed by the Discovery mission in 1989, where the crew orbited the Earth 79 times in 120 hours. His final mission on the shuttle Atlantis involved medical tests and launching a defense satellite. He retired as a Colonel in the U.S. Air Force and received several awards, including NASA's Outstanding Leadership Award.

Dr. MAE JEMISON
NASA, Chemical Engineer, Astronaut

SOME IMAGES IN THIS BOOK WERE CREATED BY CANVA AI, CRAIYON AI, AND PIXABAY POWERED BY ISTOCK

Mae Carol Jemison was born in Decatur, Alabama on October 17, 1956. She moved to Chicago and graduated from Morgan Park High School at 16. Jemison became the first African American woman astronaut after joining NASA Astronaut Group 12 in 1987.

On September 12, 1992, she flew aboard the space shuttle Endeavor, spending over a week in orbit. In addition to her space career, Jemison has written books, appeared in "Star Trek: The Next Generation," and been honored in the National

Women's Hall of Fame and the International Space Hall of Fame.

Dr. JOAN ELIZABETH HIGGINBOTHAM
NASA, Engineer, Astronaut

Higginbotham is an American engineer and a former NASA astronaut. She served as a mission specialist aboard the Space Shuttle Discovery mission STS-116. After Mae Jemison and Stephanie Wilson, she is the third African American woman to go into space.

Dr. STEPHANIE DIANA WILSON
NASA, Astronaut

Wilson is an American engineer and a NASA astronaut. She has been on three Space Shuttle missions and is the second African American woman to go into space after Mae Jemison. Her 42 days in space are the most of any African American astronaut, male or female.

NEIL DEGRASSE TYSON
Astrophysicist

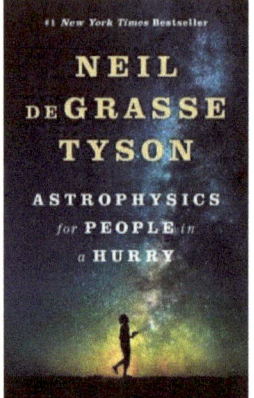

Neil deGrasse Tyson is an astronomer and astrophysicist known for making complex science accessible. He holds a master's degree in astronomy from the University of Texas (1983) and advocates for science education and space exploration. In 2004, he served on a commission examining the future of the U.S. space program.

His research includes star formation, black holes, and dwarf galaxies. In his 2020 essay, "Reflections on the Color of My Skin," Tyson discussed racial profiling with Black scientists, highlighting issues like "Driving While Black." He continues to contribute to scientific discussions today.

BENJAMIN BANNEKER
Mathematician, Astronomer, Writer, Archivist

Benjamin Banneker was born a free Black man on November 9, 1731, in Baltimore County, Maryland. He was a self-educated mathematician and astronomer known for his influential almanacs, published from 1792 to 1797. These included his astronomical calculations, opinion pieces, and helpful information for fishermen.Banneker played a vital role in surveying the District of Columbia and accurately predicted lunar and solar eclipses. He also calculated the cycle of the 17-year locust and exchanged letters with Thomas Jefferson, advocating for racial equality.

DOGON NATION
Astronomers

Astronomers from the Dogon nation have long claimed to observe a double or even triple-star system centered around Sirius. They attribute their knowledge to "instructor" gods called Nommos, described as amphibious, fish-like beings. Remarkably, the Dogon knew of Sirius and its triple system thousands of years before modern science confirmed its existence.

Studies indicate that Sirius C, the third star, is a dim red dwarf, making it difficult to detect with modern equipment. The Dogon named this star "Emme Ya". It recognized that Sirius has a planetary companion called "Po Tolo," which completes an orbit every 50 years—a fact verified by astronomers. They also referred to Jupiter as "Dana Tolo" and knew about its four satellites and rings. While Sirius was confirmed as a binary star by Alvan Clark in 1862, the Dogon had observed these celestial phenomena without modern instruments.

CHAPTER 4

MATHEMATICS

Many have been led to believe mathematics started with European colonization, but Africans had already begun building, measuring, and counting thousands of years before any European contact.

THE LEBOMBO BONE
Mathematics

The earliest measuring instrument was found in
Swaziland, Africa, which is over 40,000 years old.
Africans were already using algebra, mathematics,
and numerals. According to The Universal Book of
Mathematics, the Lebombo bones had 29 notches,
suggesting they may have been used to count the
lunar phase. It is believed that African women may
have been the first mathematicians to track
menstrual cycles. In the cases of other notched
bones, no consistent notch tally has been found
globally. The knowledge spread worldwide with the
diaspora of Africans about 30,000 BC. And to
clarify, the first mathematicians may have been
African women.

THE ISHANGO BONE
Mathematics

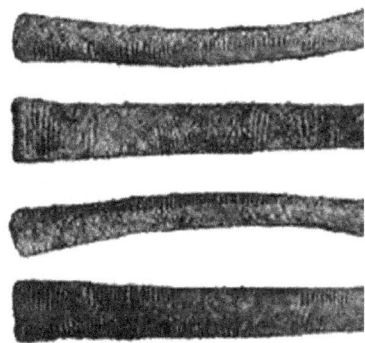

The Ishango bone is a bone tool dated to the Upper Paleolithic era. It is a dark brown bone, the fibula of a baboon, with a sharp piece of quartz affixed to one end. It could be used as a tally stick for counting or solving mathematical equations. It was found in the Democratic Republic of Congo and is estimated to be around 20,000 years old.

GEBET'A or "MANCALA" GAME
Mathematical Game

This ancient counting board game, known as Gebet or Mancala, dates back to around 700 BC and continues to be played today. It originates from Yeha, Ethiopia.

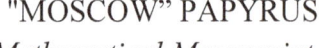

"MOSCOW" PAPYRUS
Mathematical Manuscript

The Moscow Mathematical Papyrus, from circa 2000-1800 B.C., is a hieratic script discovered in

Egypt. Named after Vladimir Golenischev, it measures 15 feet long and 3 inches wide and contains about 25 mathematical problems. This ancient document, which predates European colonization, showcases early geometry and algebra and originates from the 13th dynasty during Egypt's Second Intermediate Period, around 1850 B.C. It is older than the Rhind Mathematical Papyrus but smaller in size.

TOMBOUCTOU MANUSCRIPTS
Mathematical Manuscript

Found in Timbuktu, Mali, Africa, these mathematical and astronomical manuscripts feature art, medicine, philosophy, and science. Over 700,000 manuscripts exist in the collection.

CHAPTER 5

ARCHITECTURE

African people have a long history as builders, creating diverse structures from sculptures to sturdy walls. Their contributions range from the Great Pyramids of Giza and the rock-hewn churches of Lalibela to the mosques of Timbuktu, showcasing advanced engineering and cultural identity. Artisans craft functional objects like carved stools and jewelry, reflecting rich cultural diversity. Today, modern African architects blend traditional techniques with contemporary designs, honoring their heritage while fostering a vibrant construction scene across the continent.

Great Wall of Benin, 1460 AD

The Benin walls were a formidable system of ramparts and moats that reached heights of 20 meters (66 feet) and spanned 16,000 kilometers. Built between 800 AD and 1460 AD, they enclosed an area of 6,500 square kilometers and protected important sites, including the Royal Palace.

The inner wall, resembling a two-story building, surrounded key sites and featured a guarded entrance where travelers paid a toll. The outer walls encompassed the upper city, home to the Uzama chiefs and Army commander, with strict security limiting access to the king. In 1674, Portuguese captain Lorenzo Pinto described the town as larger than Lisbon and well-organized, with its defenses helping to shield the people from the Transatlantic Slave Trade.

ADAMS CALENDAR
South Africa
World's Oldest Timepiece 75,000 years old

The Adams Clock is a series of ancient circular monolithic stone structures in Mpumalanga, South Africa. It is believed to be approximately 75,000 years old, predating any other structure on Earth. Archaeologists estimate that the site has well over a million ancient stone ruins. Various tools and artifacts have been recovered from these ruins, indicating an extended settlement that spanned over 200,000 years. The most spectacular example of these ancient ruins is called Adam's Calendar. This stunning ancient site is aligned with the cardinal points of north, south, east, and west, as well as the solstices and equinoxes. A pilot rediscovered the calendar in 2003 and named it Adam's Calendar because it is possibly the oldest structure on earth linked to the human species.

NUBIAN PYRAMIDS
Pyramids between 2,500 B.C. and 300 A.D

The Nubian pyramids were built by the rulers of the ancient Kushite kingdoms between 2,500 B.C. and 300 A.D. Made from stepped horizontally positioned stone blocks, the pyramids range from 20 to 98 feet high but rise from relatively small footprints that rarely exceed 26 feet in width, making them exceptionally steep. Nubia is an area of the Nile Valley in the northern section of present-day Sudan.

HEREMAKHET or HERU-EM-AKHET *The Sphinx*
2530 BC

Best known by its Greek name, the "Sphinx" of Giza is one of the world's largest and most recognizable statues. The half-human, half-lion stone was sculpted by Africans some 4,500 years ago. The Sphinx was built in approximately 2530 BC by the pharaoh Khafre (the 4th king of the Fourth Dynasty, c. 2575–c. 2465 BC) and the people of his time. Recent findings and calculations by scientists believe that this is the face of an African woman.

The Great Pyramids of Giza
2600-2100 BCE

Skilled African Egyptian laborers primarily built the pyramids, not slaves as once believed. Many workers were local farmers who contributed during the Nile's flood season when farming paused. Constructed during the Old Kingdom (circa 2600-2100 BCE) by kings such as Cheops, Khafre, and Menkaure, the workforce comprised paid laborers and skilled craftsmen, underscoring Egypt's complex social structure.

Additionally, Nubian kingdoms in Sudan built pyramids between 2700 and 2300 years ago, with Kushite pharaohs, such as Taharqa, leaving an architectural legacy. Modern scholarship emphasizes the cultural diversity of ancient Egypt, highlighting the brilliance of this civilization in terms of its technological and organizational achievements.

TIMBUKTU
Founded around 1100 CE

Timbuktu is an ancient city in Mali, located about 20 kilometers (12 miles) north of the Niger River. Founded around 1100 CE, it became a key trading hub on the trans-Saharan caravan route and an Islamic culture center. By the 14th to 16th centuries, it was an important intellectual and cultural center, renowned for its manuscripts, considered the "single most important collection from pre-colonial West Africa," according to Duke University scholar Bruce Hall. Timbuktu was designated a UNESCO World Heritage site in 1988.

THE SALADIN CITADEL1176 and 1183 AD
Citadel

This medieval Islamic fortification stands in Cairo, Egypt. The Ayyubid ruler Salah al-Din (Saladin) fortified the Citadel between 1176 and 1183 AD to protect Cairo from the Crusaders.

FASIL GHEBBI17th and 18th centuries
Fortress-City

 This fortress city within Gondar, Ethiopia, was founded in the 17th and 18th centuries by Emperor Fasilides (Fasil). It was the seat of Ethiopia's emperors. Covering an area of about 750,000 square feet, it is surrounded by a 3,000-foot-long wall and encloses more than a dozen) buildings, including the kingdom's treasury building, three churches, stables, a banquet hall, Gondar Castle, a separate castle for the empress, and other gathering spaces. Fasil Ghebbi features unique architecture with diverse influences, including Nubian styles.

ELMINA CASTLE1482
Castle

The Portuguese erected the castle in 1482 as São Jorge da Elmina Mina Castle, also known simply as Mina or Feitoria da Mina in present-day Elmina, Ghana (formerly the Gold Coast). First established as a trade settlement, the castle later became one of the most significant stops on the route of the Atlantic slave trade, known as "The point of no return." The country of Ghana has reclaimed the castle for historical purposes.

THE AFRICAN RENAISSANCE MONUMENT
Monument April 03, 2010

The African Renaissance Monument is a 161-foot-high bronze statue on a hill in Dakar, Senegal. The representation of an African man, woman, and child emerging from a volcano facing the sea. It was the idea of former President Abdoulaye Wade of Senegal and was revealed on April 03, 2010.

Great Zimbabwe
11th century and continued until the 15th century
Monuments.

Great Zimbabwe is a ruined city near Lake Mutirikwe and Masvingo in southeastern Zimbabwe. It was the capital of the Kingdom of Zimbabwe during the Late Iron Age. Construction by the Shona people began in the 11th century and continued until the 15th century, covering 1,780 acres and accommodating up to 18,000 people.

As one of the largest man-made structures in the world, Great Zimbabwe boasts impressive walls, some exceeding five meters in height, built without the use of mortar. Vicente Pegado, captain of the Portuguese garrison in Sofala, first mentioned the ruins in 1531.

ROBERT ROBINSON TAYLOR
Architect

Taylor is widely regarded as the first academically trained and credentialed Black architect in America. He attended the Massachusetts Institute of Technology, where his final bachelor's degree project in Architecture was "Design for a Soldiers' Home," a housing to accommodate aging Civil War veterans. Booker T. Washington recruited him to help establish the Tuskegee Institute in Alabama. This campus is now associated with Taylor's work.

MOSES McKISSACK III Of Mckissack &
Mckissack
Architectural firm

McKissack was a master builder in Nashville, TN.
In 1905, he joined his brother Calvin to found one
of the earliest black architectural firms in the United
States: McKissack & McKissack. In 1942,
McKissack & McKissack was awarded a $5.7
million contract to design and build the 99th Pursuit
Squadron Airbase in Tuskegee, AL. It was the most
significant federal contract ever given to an African
American firm. Fifth-generation McKissack family
architect/builder Deryl McKissack manages the
current McKissack & McKissack design firm.

JULIAN ABELE
Architect

Abele was one of America's most essential yet anonymous architects. He was the first black graduate to hold an architecture degree from the University of Pennsylvania in 1902. He never signed his work and was never publicly acknowledged in his lifetime. Abele spent his entire career at the Philadelphia firm of the Gilded Age architect Horace Trumbauer. During his tenure at the Trumbauer firm, Abele worked on the expansion of the Duke University campus, a whites-only university in Durham, North Carolina.

NORMA MERRICK SKLAREK
Architect

Sklarek was the first Black woman to become a licensed architect in New York (1954) and California (1962). She was also the first Black woman to become a fellow of the American Institute of Architecture (1966 FAIA). She participated in many projects, most notably overseeing a design team headed by the Argentine architect César Pelli.

DAVID ADJAYE
Architect

Sir David Adjaye Obe is an award-winning Ghanaian architect known for his ingenious use of material. 2000 David founded Adjaye Associates, which operates globally and takes on many challenging projects. The firm's work ranges from private houses to major art centers and civic buildings. Its most significant project to date, in collaboration with the Freelon group, Davis Brody Bond LLP, and Smith Group JJR Architectures, was the National Museum of African American History and Culture in Washington, DC, on the National Mall in 2016. It was named the National Mall in 2016 and Cultural Event of the Year by the New York Times.

CHAPTER 6

CIVIL RIGHTS LEADERS, SCHOLARS & MASTER TEACHERS

Many have fought against injustices worldwide, doing so in various ways, including through legal systems, marches, protests, and literature. Many continue the fight for human and civil rights and justice today. Black African scholars and master teachers have researched history to find the African identity in the world.

ALEXANDER DUMAS
(1802-1870)

Alexandre Dumas was a famous French author born to a mixed-heritage family. His father, Thomas-Alexandre Dumas, was of African descent and a former enslaved person. Dumas rose to fame in the 1840s with classics like "The Three Musketeers" and "The Count of Monte Cristo." His novel "Georges" addressed racism and colonialism, reflecting his background. Despite facing racial prejudice, he became a beloved literary figure and was reinterred in the Panthéon in Paris in 2002, alongside other greats like Victor Hugo.

ALEXANDER PUSHKIN
Literature author poet

Alexander Pushkin, a pivotal Russian poet from 1799 to 1837, is a foundational figure in Russian literature, known for his African ancestry explored in "Peter the Great's Negro." He modernized the Russian language and transformed literature by incorporating vernacular speech and blending genres. Pushkin's most notable work, "Eugene Onegin," is considered the first great Russian novel, significantly influencing later fiction. His passionate life was cut short by a duel, but he remains a literary pioneer who inspired generations with his emotional narrative style.

Dr. MARTIN LUTHER KING, JR.
Civil Rights Activist

Dr. King was a Baptist minister and civil rights activist. He is most famous for his "I Have a Dream" speech and his powerful impact on race relations in the United States, beginning in the mid-1950s. King headed the Southern Christian Leadership Conference (SCLC). Through his activism and inspirational speeches, he played a pivotal role in ending the legal segregation of black citizens in the United States, as well as the creation of the Civil Rights Act of 1964 and the Voting Rights Act of 1965. King won honors, including the Nobel Peace Prize in 1964. He remains remembered as one of history's most influential and inspirational African American leaders. In the last years of his life, King boldly forged a radical, multi-racial movement for economic justice.

MARCUS GARVEY
Civil Rights Activist

Marcus Garvey was born in St. Ann's Bay, Jamaica, and began his career as a printer's apprentice. He worked as a newspaper editor in Central America, highlighting the exploitation of migrant workers. After moving to London and studying at Birkbeck College, he returned to Jamaica and, in August 1914, co-founded the Universal Negro Improvement Association (UNIA), aiming to establish a black-governed nation in Africa. In 1916, Garvey moved to the United States, expanding the UNIA in Harlem and other urban areas, promoting a proud black identity and an independent black economy.

He founded the Negro Factories Corporation, the Black Star Line, and various businesses. Garvey inspired African descendants globally, introducing a flag symbolizing pride, red representing the struggle for redemption, black signifying the noble race, and green symbolizing Africa's vegetation. These colors are still celebrated today.

HARRIET TUBMAN
Abolitionist

Harriet Tubman, born Araminta Ross in Dorchester County, Maryland, was a courageous conductor of the Underground Railroad. She dedicated her life to freeing enslaved individuals and fighting for social justice. Born into slavery, she escaped and led at least thirteen missions, rescuing around seventy enslaved people.

Known for her unwavering determination, she famously declared, "You'll be free or die," ensuring none turned back. During the Civil War, she served as a scout, spy, nurse, and cook for the Union. Tubman's lifelong fight for freedom and justice made her an enduring symbol of courage and resistance.

MINISTER LOUIS FARRAKHAN
Human rights leader

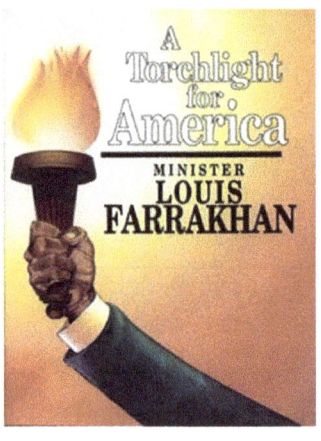

Born Louis Eugene Walcott, Louis Farrakhan was a talented musician and athlete. He graduated from Boston English High School, attended Winston-Salem Teacher's College, and recorded calypso albums as "The Charmer." 1953 he married Khadijah Farrakhan and left college to support her during her pregnancy. Farrakhan joined the Nation of Islam in 1955 and became the minister of Temple No. 11 in Boston the following year. He focused on improving the Harlem community and combating negative stereotypes of African American men, organizing the Million Man March in 1995 and the Millions More Movement in 2005. He was named Person of the Year by Black Entertainment Television in 2005 and ranked fifth in the AP-AOL "Black Voices" poll in 2006.

JESSE LOUIS JACKSON, SR.
Civil Rights Activist

Jackson is an American civil rights activist and Baptist minister. He was a candidate for the Democratic presidential nomination in 1984 and 1988 and served as a shadow U.S. Senator for the District of Columbia from 1991 to 1997. He is the founder of Rainbow/PUSH, a nonprofit organization formed as a merger of Operation PUSH (People United to Save Humanity) and the National Rainbow Coalition. The organizations pursue social justice, civil rights, and political activism.

ALFRED CHARLES "Al" SHARPTON, JR.
Civil Rights Activist

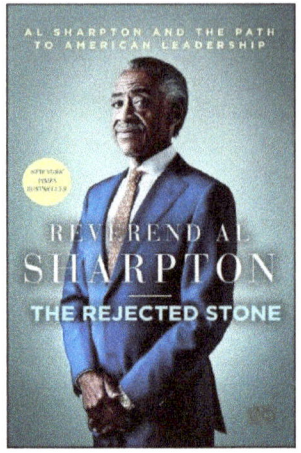

Sharpton is an American Baptist minister, civil rights activist, television/radio talk show host, and trusted White House adviser to President Barack Obama. According to 60 Minutes, Sharpton has "become the president's go-to black leader." He is a former candidate for the Democratic nomination for the U.S. presidential election and is known for fighting for racial equality and justice for African Americans.

MALCOLM X
Civil Rights Activist

Malcolm X, born Malcolm Little and later known as El-Hajj Malik El-Shabazz, was a Muslim minister and human rights activist. From 1946 to 1952, he converted to Islam and joined the Nation of Islam, an African American movement blending Islam with black nationalism. Rising quickly, he organized temples across several cities and became minister of Harlem's Temple No. 7. A powerful speaker and organizer, he voiced the frustrations of Black Americans during the civil rights era. In 1964, he left the Nation, founded Muslim Mosque, Inc., and embraced Sunni Islam after a pilgrimage to Mecca. He later established the Organization of Afro-American Unity to advocate for global human rights.

FREDERICK DOUGLASS
Social Reformer and founder of the Abolitionist Movement

Frederick Douglass escaped slavery in 1838, adopting his surname to evade capture. A talented writer and abolitionist, he authored *The Life and Times of Frederick Douglass* and founded the anti-slavery newspaper *North Star*. During the Civil War, he advised President Lincoln on arming former slaves. He held several significant government positions, including U.S. Marshal for the District of Columbia and U.S. Minister to Haiti. Douglass was also a strong supporter of women's rights.

SOJOURNER TRUTH
Abolitionist, Women's Rights Activist

Born Isabella Baumfree, Sojourner Truth became a key abolitionist and women's rights activist after changing her name in 1843. In 1851, she delivered her famous "Ain't I a Woman?" speech at the Ohio Women's Rights Convention.

"Well, children, where there is so much noise, something must be wrong. The Black people of the South and the women of the North are all talking about rights, and the white men will soon find themselves in a difficult position.
One man thinks women need help getting into carriages. Nobody ever helps me! And ain't I a woman? I have worked hard and was born to

thirteen children, most sold into slavery. When I cried in grief, only Jesus heard me.

They say intellect matters, but what does that have to do with rights? If my cup holds a pint and yours a quart, wouldn't it be unfair not to let me have my share?

Some say women can't have rights because Christ wasn't a woman. But where did Christ come from? From God and a woman! Man had nothing to do with Him.

If the first woman could change the world, these women can, together, set things right again. Now that they're asking, men better let them.

Thank you for listening; old Sojourner has nothing more to say."

IDA BELL WELLS-BARNETT aka LoLa
Journalist, Civil Rights Leader

Ida B. Wells-Barnett was a trailblazing African American civil rights activist, investigative journalist, and suffragist from Mississippi. Educated at Rust and Fisk Universities, she gained notoriety in 1884 for refusing to give up her train seat—an act of defiance that predated Rosa Parks by 71 years. She won a $500 settlement from the railroad but had to pay court costs.

As co-owner and editor of "The Free Speech and Headlight," starting in 1889, she wrote impactful anti-segregation editorials under the pseudonym "Lola." Following the lynching of her friends, she urged the Memphis Black community to leave the city, resulting in the exodus of over 6,000 people and boycotts of white businesses. Wells-Barnett later moved to New York and Chicago, continuing her anti-lynching efforts through journalism and lectures in Britain. She was a key figure in establishing the NAACP alongside W.E.B. Du Bois and others, and in 1909, she became one of the first Black women to run for public office in the Illinois State Legislature.

DR. GEORGE FRASER
Entrepreneur, author, and motivational speaker.

Fraser is an entrepreneur, author, and motivational speaker. He studied at New York University (NYU) and earned his degree from Dartmouth's Tuck School of Business. Fraser spent 17 years in management at Procter & Gamble and Ford. His 1994 book, "Success Runs in Our Race," became a bestseller, and his follow-up book, "Race for Success," was recognized as one of the top business books of 1999 by Booklist. Additionally, Fraser created the "SuccessGuide" series, which focuses on Black resources. Among his many accolades, he holds a Guinness World Record for organizing the most significant balloon release, with 1.4 million balloons, while working with United Way of Cleveland in 1986.

ALFRED BOWMAN "DR. SEBI"
Master herbalist and Engineer

Alfred Bowman, better known as Dr. Sebi Bowman, although without formal medical training, was an Honduran herbalist and self-proclaimed healer who also practiced in the United States for decades, starting in the late 1980s. Bowman claimed to cure all diseases with herbs and with a vegan diet. Numerous entertainment and acting celebrities were among his clients. He was arrested and accused by the state of New York of practicing medicine without a license. After the trial, Bowman was acquitted and found innocent, and by the definition of medicine, he could not claim his work as a cure. Dr. Sebi continued to practice herbalism in Usha village until his death in May 2016.

ROSA LOUISE McCAULEY PARKS
Civil Rights Activist

In December 1943, Rosa Parks joined the Montgomery chapter of the NAACP as chapter secretary. Her act of defiance in 1955, refusing to give up her bus seat to a white man, sparked the civil rights movement and led to the Montgomery Bus Boycott. The boycott lasted over a year, concluding when the Supreme Court declared bus segregation unconstitutional. After facing harassment, Parks moved to Detroit, where she worked as an administrative aide for Congressman John Conyers Jr. until her retirement in 1988. She authored "Rosa Parks: My Story" and received the Congressional Gold Medal in 1999, earning titles like "The First Lady of Civil Rights."

Dr. WILLIAM EDWARD BURGHARDT
"W. E. B." Du BOIS
American Sociologist, Historian, Civil Rights Activist, Pan-Africanist, Author, Editor

W.E.B. Du Bois was an early advocate for using data to address social issues in the black community. His influential work, The Souls of Black Folk, became essential reading in African American studies. Du Bois began writing for the New York Globe and Freeman in 1883 and received advanced degrees in history from Harvard in 1888. He pursued a Ph.D. at the University of Berlin, producing his first book, "The Suppression of the African Slave Trade to the United States of America, 1638–1870," which became a standard educational text. His statistical study of Philadelphia's Seventh Ward is among the earliest sociological works. While at Atlanta University, he taught sociology and continued his research, including work on The Souls of Black Folk. In 1910, Du Bois became the director of the

NAACP and later moved to Ghana, where he conceived the Encyclopedia Africana to unify the African diaspora.

ARTURO ALFONSO SCHOMBURG
African-Puerto Rican Historian, Writer, Activist

Schomburg was a prominent Afro-Puerto Rican historian, writer, and activist who assembled an extensive collection of art, literature, and artifacts about African Americans during the Harlem Renaissance. This literary movement originated in Harlem between 1917 and 1935, a time when Americans began to recognize the richness of African American folklore and writings.

MEDGAR WILEY EVERS
Civil Rights Activist

Evers was drafted into the U.S. Army in 1943. He fought in both France and Germany during World War II and received an honorable discharge in 1946. In 1954, Evers became the first field secretary for the NAACP in Mississippi. Evers also led demonstrations and economic boycotts of white-owned companies that practiced discrimination. Evers called for a new investigation into the 1955 lynching of Emmett Till, a 14-year-old African American boy who had allegedly been killed for talking to a white woman.

KWAME TURE, a.k.a. STOKELEY CARMICHAEL
Civil Rights Activist

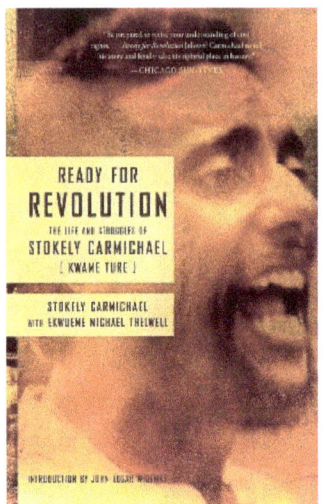

Kwame Ture was a civil rights activist during the 1960s Civil Rights Movement and, later, the global Pan-African and Black Power movements. Kwame was a leader of the Student Nonviolent Coordinating Committee, "Honorary Prime Minister" of the Black Panther Party, and a leader of the All-African People's Revolutionary Party. As of now, Bobby Seal, co-founder of the Black Panther Party

BOBBY SEALE
Black Panther Party

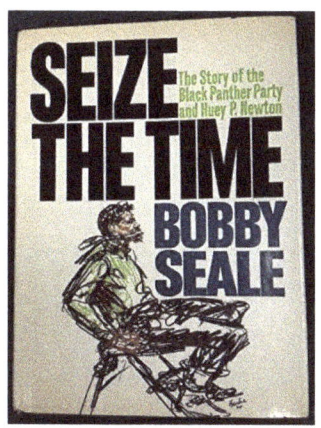

He is best known as a co-founder of the Black Panther Party (BPP), which was created in 1966 to address police brutality and racial injustice in African American communities. Born in Dallas, Texas, in 1936, he partnered with Huey P. Newton to form the party, which became famous for its militant stance and social programs like complimentary breakfasts and health clinics. Seale also gained attention for his involvement in the Chicago Eight trial in 1968, where he was charged with conspiracy and inciting a riot during protests at the Democratic National Convention. Though the BPP declined in the early 1970s due to internal conflict and government pressure, Seale continued to advocate for social justice. His legacy remains tied to the fight for black empowerment and equality. Bobby Seale is still alive. He was born on October 22, 1936, and continues to be recognized as a significant figure in the civil rights movement and Black empowerment.

HUEY P NEWTON
Political activist and c
o-founder of the Black Panther Party

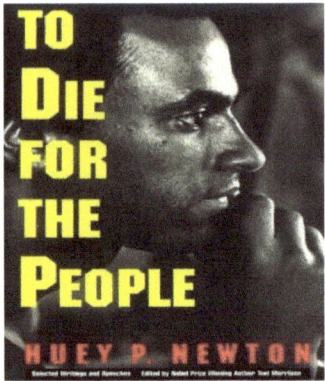

Huey P. Newton (1942–1989) was an American political activist and co-founder of the Black Panther Party (BPP), established in 1966 in Oakland, California. The BPP aimed to combat police brutality and systemic racism while promoting Black civil rights and community empowerment. Newton was involved in initiatives like free breakfast programs for children and health clinics. As a symbol of resistance against racial oppression, he was arrested and convicted for the death of a police officer in 1967, but this conviction was later overturned. Newton's activism and legal struggles kept him in the public eye until he died in 1989, helping to highlight issues of racial injustice and inequality in the United States.

Dr. JAWANZA KUNJUFU
Educational Consultant, Author

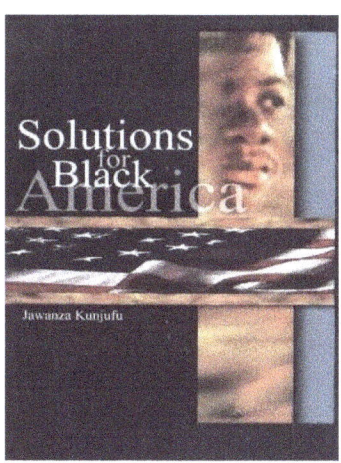

Kunjufu is an educational consultant, author, and video and film producer. He has dedicated his career to addressing the ills afflicting black culture in the United States, working primarily as an educational consultant and author but more recently expanding into video and film production. He is the founder and president of African American Images, a Chicago-based publishing company. Kunjufu was early on fascinated—and appalled—by the educational system for black students in America, and from 1974 onward, he began delivering lectures and workshops treating the problems facing black educators. He was known for teaching young African American youth productive social skills with each other and outside the communities. In 1982, he authored *Countering the Conspiracy to Destroy Black Boys.*

MARY JANE McLEOD BETHUNE
American Educator and Civil Rights Leader

Mary McLeod Bethune, born to former slaves, graduated from Scotia Seminary in 1893 and founded the Daytona Normal and Industrial Institute in 1904, now Bethune-Cookman College. She established the National Council of Negro Women in 1935 and served as an advisor to President Franklin D. Roosevelt on minority affairs. After her death, she was honored with induction into the National Women's Hall of Fame in 1973 and a U.S. Postal Service stamp in 1985.

Dr. WHITNEY MOORE YOUNG, JR.
Civil Rights Leader

Whitney M. Young, Jr. (1921-1971) was a pivotal civil rights leader who advocated racial integration. He served in World War II, earned a master's degree in social work, and led the Omaha branch of the Urban League. As dean of the School of Social Work at Atlanta University, he was active in the Civil Rights Movement and was an adviser to President Lyndon B. Johnson, receiving the Presidential Medal of Freedom in 1968. Young also authored two influential books and wrote a syndicated newspaper column.

JAMES EARL CHANEY
Civil Rights Activist

 J.E. Chaney was from Meridian, Mississippi. He was an early supporter for civil and voting rights. He was one of three American civil rights workers who were murdered during Freedom Summer by members of the Ku Klux Klan near Philadelphia, Mississippi. The others were Andrew Goodman and Michael Schwerner from New York City. Outrage over the activists' disappearances helped gain passage of the Civil Rights Act of 1964. 41 years after the murders, white supremacist Edgar Ray Killen was charged by the state of Mississippi for his part in the crimes. In 2005, he was convicted of three manslaughter counts and was given a 60-year sentence.

CORETTA SCOTT KING
Civil Rights Activist and Leader

King was an American author, activist, singer, and civil rights leader. The widow of Martin Luther King, Jr., Coretta Scott King, helped lead the African American Civil Rights Movement in the 1960s. King often participated in her husband's exploits and goals. She also often used music to spread her messages.

RICHARD CLAXTON "DICK" GREGORY
Comedian, Social Activist

Dick Gregory, born in St. Louis, Missouri, was a comedian, social activist, writer, conspiracy theorist, and entrepreneur. After serving in the Army and graduating from Southern Illinois State University, he found success in comedy, with a significant break in 1961 at Hugh Hefner's Playboy Club.

An active participant in the Civil Rights Movement, Gregory formed friendships with leaders like Dr. Martin Luther King Jr. He later advocated health and fitness, promoting a vegetarian diet and nutritional awareness in Black communities. After his cancer diagnosis in 1999, he opted for dietary changes over chemotherapy, resulting in remission. Gregory is celebrated as a groundbreaking figure in Black history.

Dr. ASA G. HILLIARD III
Professor, Historian

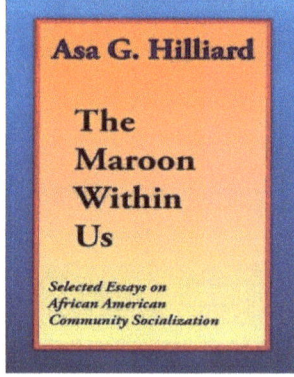

Hilliard, a.k.a. Nana Baffour Amankwatia II, was an African American professor of educational psychology who began working on Indigenous ancient African history, culture, education, and society in the early 1960s.

Dr. Edward W. Robinson, Jr.
Attorney, historian, author, and professor

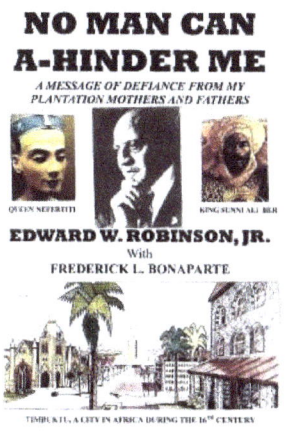

Dr. Robinson, author of *African Genesis Science*, demonstrated Africa's foundational contributions to mathematics, science, and civilization. As an attorney, historian, and professor, he led Philadelphia's African Studies Committee and co-authored significant works, including *Journey of the Songhai People* (1970). He created various cultural works, including the *Black Rhapsody* album and *The Songhai Princess* animation. Robinson developed an art gallery of notable African and African American figures and advanced the African Genesis theory to address racial bias through education and media highlighting African cultural heritage.

ANGELA YVONNE DAVIS
Political Activist

Davis is an American political activist, scholar, and author who led the American Communist Party in the 1960s. Writer, activist, and educator Angela Davis was born on January 26, 1944, in Birmingham, Alabama. She grew up in a middle-class neighborhood dubbed "Dynamite Hill" due to many of the African American homes in the area that the Ku Klux Klan bombed. Davis is best known as a radical African American educator and activist for civil rights and other social issues. She learned about racial prejudice from her experiences with discrimination growing up in Alabama. As a teenager, Davis organized study groups, which were broken up by the authorities.

DR. JOHN HENRIK CLARKE
Educator, Historian, and Author

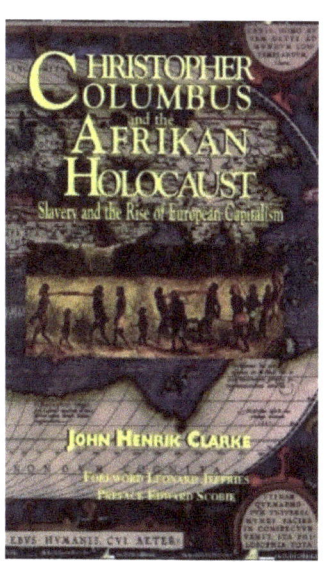

John Henry Clark was born in the South and moved north to Harlem, NY, in 1933 as a part of the Great Migration of rural blacks from the South to northern cities. In New York, he pursued scholarship and activism. He renamed himself as John Henrik and added an "e" to his surname, spelling it as "Clarke." Clarke studied intermittently at New York University, Columbia University, Hunter College, the New School of Social Research, and Professional Writers. From 1969 to 1986, Dr. Clarke was a Black and Puerto Rican Studies professor at Hunter College of the City University of New York, In 1968. He founded the African Heritage Studies Association and the Black Caucus of the African Studies Association. Dr. Clarke advocated for studies of the African American experience by challenging the views of academic historians and helped shift the way African history was studied and taught. Along with Leonard Jeffries, Dr. Clarke was the founder and

first president of the African Heritage Studies
Association, supporting scholars in history, culture,
literature, and the arts.

Dr. LEONARD JEFFRIES
Scholar, Activist

Dr. Leonard Jeffries
is a founding
director and a former
President of the
Association for the
Study of Classical
African Civilizations
(ASCAC). Known
for his African-
Centred scholarship,
achieved national
prominence in the
early 1990s. Jeffries
took his first trip to
Africa with the
Crossroads program. His leadership abilities and
proficiency in French made him an asset to the
program. By the summer of 1962, he became the
group leader of a trip to Senegal. His scholastic
exploits have taken him to Ghana, Brazil,
Switzerland, and throughout the Caribbean.

135

He worked on his Ph.D. in the Ivory Coast, studying economics and politics, and became known outside his field in 1987 when he was on a state task force to fight racism in the public-school curriculum. He was recently appointed the International Executive Director of the Organization of Afro-American Unity (O.A.A.U.), founded in 1964 by El-Hajj Malik El-Shabazz (Malcolm X).

Dr. FRANCES CRESS WELSING
Psychiatrist, Master Teacher, and Author

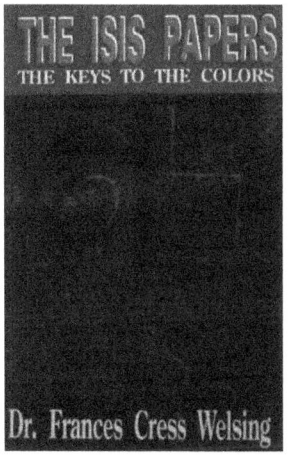

In the 1960s, Dr. Welsing worked at many hospitals as a psychiatrist, including hospitals for children. Welsing studied the effects of white supremacy on the black community. As an assistant professor at Howard University, she formulated her first body of work in 1969, *The Cress Theory of Color-Confrontation*, which she self-published in 1970 as an introduction to her thoughts that would be developed later into *The ISIS Papers*

(1991), a compilation of essays about global and local race relations.

PROF. JAMES SMALLS
Master Teacher, Educator of Religious and African Spiritual System

"If you give up your fear of death you can never be made a slave again, but as long as you fear death you can be made a slave! And the only reason you fear death is because you are ignorant to the fact you can never die!" – Prof. James Small

Professor James Smalls is an expert in African traditional spirituality. Since the 1960s, he has been involved in several black liberation movements. He has taught for over 35 years, including at New York Technical College, where he taught African studies, history, and culture. Smalls currently lectures around the world about African history and traditions.

THE HONORABLE ELIJAH MUHAMMAD
The leader of the Nation

Elijah Muhammad (born Robert Poole) left home at 16 and settled in Detroit in 1923, where he worked on a Chevrolet assembly line. He and his brothers became followers of W.D. Fard, the Nation of Islam's founder. Muhammad quickly rose through the organization's ranks, emphasizing African American self-help and education. After moving to Chicago, he expanded the movement by establishing the Temple of Islam, the Muhammad Speaks newspaper, and the University of Islam (a private school system). The organization grew to include movement-owned businesses, apartment buildings, and farms to produce ritually acceptable food. Muhammad instituted strict guidelines for members, including dietary restrictions (no pork), bans on alcohol and smoking, dress codes, and prohibitions against gambling, profanity, and certain forms of entertainment. Members were also required to abandon their "slave names."

Muhammad, who revised the movement's theology and authored several influential books, led the Nation of Islam during its incredible growth in the mid-20th century.

DR. YOSEF ALFREDO ANTONIO BEN-JOCHANNAN
Master Teacher, Educator, Historian and Author

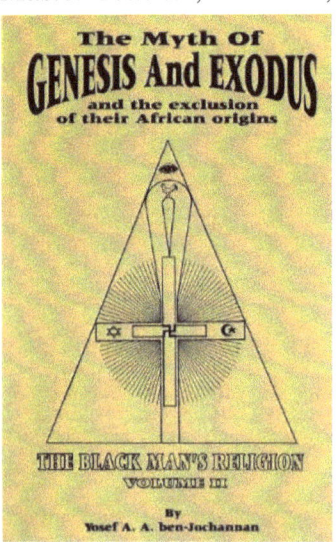

Professor Yosef Ben-Jochannan, born December 21, 1918, in a Falasha community in Ethiopia, obtained several degrees before coming to America. In 1938 and 1939, Dr. Ben earned a Bachelor of Science in Civil Engineering at the University of Puerto Rico as well as a degree in Architectural Engineering from the University of Havana, Cuba. He received doctoral degrees in Cultural

Anthropology and Moorish History from the University of Havana and the University of Barcelona, Spain. After his arrival in America, he taught at Cornell University for over 15 years and lectured widely on both sides of the Atlantic. His theme was the ancient civilizations of Egypt. His presentations were popular with African descendants. He emphasized on African contributions to the world. He authored 49 books, primarily on ancient Nile Valley civilizations and their impact on Western cultures, including "Black Man of the Nile and His Family." Before his death, Dr. Ben passed many of his works on to the nation of Islam. "

 DR. LLAILA O. AFRIKA and DR. MELANIE STEVENSON
Holistic Health Doctors

Drs. Afrika and Stevenson were pioneering holistic health practitioners who taught comprehensive wellness, covering relationships, nutrition, sexuality, education, parenting, and natural healing. Dr. Afrika, who passed away in March 2020, held credentials in naturopathy, nursing, acupuncture, and herbalism. With over 45 years of experience in ethnomedicine, he worked as a U.S. Army Social Worker, nurse, and Psychotherapist while advocating that good health is a universal human right. His wife, Dr. Melanie Stevenson, continues their work at their Holistic Therapies and Education Center in Indianapolis. She brings over 12 years of experience as a licensed Holistic Naturopath Practitioner specializing in health sciences, spirituality, and arts.

NELSON MANDELA
Anti-apartheid Revolutionary Political Leader

"Do not judge me by my success, judge me by how many times I fell down and got back up again."
- Nelson Mandela

Nelson Mandela was a transformative South African leader who fought against apartheid. After being imprisoned for 18 years on Robben Island following the 1963 Rivonia Trial, he was released in 1990 and worked with President de Klerk to end apartheid. He became South Africa's first black president in 1994, received the Nobel Peace Prize, and championed justice and human dignity through his philosophy of Ubuntu.

Dr. CHEIKH ANTA DIOP
Master Teacher of Pan African Studies, Author
" The African Origin of Civilization: Myth or Reality"

Cheikh Anta Diop was born in Diourbel, Senegal,

on December 29, 1923. At 23, he moved to Paris to study physics but shifted his focus to the African origins of humanity and civilization. His doctoral dissertation, which argued that ancient Egypt was an African civilization, was initially rejected but published in 1955 as "Nations Nègres et Culture." In 1960, he published two important works: "The Cultural Unity of Black Africa" and "Precolonial Black Africa." Diop was also a political activist, serving as Secretary-General of the Rassemblement Démocratique Africain (RDA) and helping to establish the first Pan-African Student Congress in Paris. He founded a radiocarbon laboratory in Dakar in 1974 and, with Théophile Obenga, reaffirmed the African origins of pharaonic Egypt at a UNESCO symposium in Cairo. His final major work, "Civilization or Barbarism: An Authentic Anthropology," was published in 1981. Diop is recognized as one of his time's leading historians, Egyptologists, linguists, and anthropologists.

Dr. CHANCELLOR WILLIAMS
Master Teacher, Historian, Sociologist, Author

""The Destruction of Black Civilization: Great Issues of a Race From 4500 B.C. to 2000 A.D."

Williams, born on December 22, 1898, in Bennettsville, South Carolina, was the son of a former slave. He earned his bachelor's degree in education and master's in history from Howard University, where he began teaching in 1946. He completed his Ph.D. in Sociology at American University in 1949 and conducted research at several prestigious institutions, including Oxford University and the

University of Chicago. Williams aimed to restore the reputation of sub-Saharan Africans before European conquests by highlighting their achievements and challenging the biases of white academics. He held various roles throughout his career, including Census Bureau worker, statistician, restaurateur, and educator.

DR. IVAN VAN SERTIMA
Master Teacher, Author
"They Came Before Columbus"

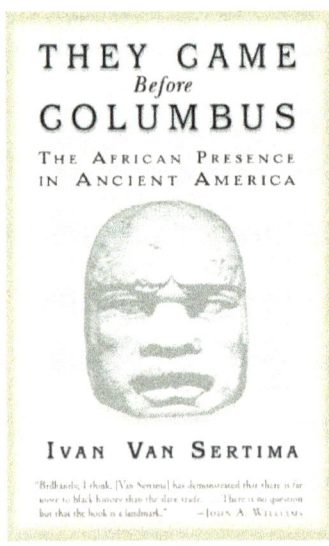

Dr. Ivan Van Sertima, born in Guyana, South America, is a notable literary critic, linguist, and anthropologist. He studied at the School of Oriental and African Studies, London University, and the Rutgers Graduate School, earning degrees in African Studies and Anthropology. From 1957 to 1959, he worked as a Press and

Broadcasting Officer in the Guyana Information
Services and later served on the Nobel Committee
for the Swedish Academy, nominating candidates
for the Nobel Prize in Literature from 1976 to 1980.
As the founding Editor of the Journal of African
Civilizations, established in 1979, he has published
influential anthologies that have shaped
multicultural education in the U.S. His poetry
appeared in "River and the Wall" (1953). Van
Sertima has lectured at over 100 universities across
the U.S., Canada, the Caribbean, South America,
and Europe. In 1987, Congress invited him to
challenge the Columbus myth, and in 1991, he
presented his thesis on the African presence in pre-
Columbian America at the Smithsonian, articulating
his findings on behalf of people of color worldwide.

Dr. GEORGE G.M. JAMES
Historian, Author

"Stolen Legacy"

James was born in British Guiana (now Guyana) in the late 19th century. He earned two bachelor's degrees and a master's degree from Durham University and likely obtained a PhD in Classics from Columbia University. He also received a teaching certificate in New York State, enabling him to teach mathematics, Latin, and Greek.

James served as a Professor of Logic and Greek at Livingstone College in North Carolina before moving to Arkansas AM&N College. In 1954, he published "Stolen Legacy," arguing that ancient Greek philosophy borrowed many ideas from ancient Egyptians without proper acknowledgment. This work significantly influenced the Afrocentric interpretation of history.

Dr. RUNOKO RASHIDI
Master Teacher, Anthropologist, Author
"The African Presence in Early Europe"

Rashidi is an anthropologist and historian focusing on the Global African Presence (Africans outside of Africa before and after enslavement). As a researcher, Dr. Rashidi has visited 120 countries and has spoken in 65 countries. He has worked with and under some of the most distinguished modern scholars, including Ivan Van Sertima, John Henrik Clarke, Asa G. Hilliard, Edward Scobie, John G. Jackson, Jan Carew, and Yosef ben-Jochannan. In 2005, Rashidi was awarded an Honorary Doctorate by the Amen-Ra Theological Seminary in Los Angeles. He is pursuing significant work on the African presence in museums worldwide.

BOOKER T. WASHINGTON
Educator, Author, Orator, Advisor to Presidents of the United States
"Up from History: The Life of Booker T. Washington"

Born into slavery, Booker T. Washington put himself through school and became a teacher after the Civil War. In 1881, he founded the Tuskegee Normal and Industrial Institute in Alabama (now known as Tuskegee University), which focused on training African Americans in agricultural pursuits. Under Washington's leadership, Tuskegee became a leading school in the country. At his death, it had more than 100 well-equipped buildings, 1,500 students, a 200-member faculty teaching 38 trades and professions, and a nearly $2 million endowment in 1901, President Theodore Roosevelt invited Washington to the White House, making him the first African American to be so honored. President Roosevelt and his successor, President William Howard Taft, used Washington as an adviser on racial matters.

DR. CLAUD ANDERSON

Master teacher, Entrepreneur, Author
State Coordinator of Education (Florida), President
of The Harvest Institute, "PowerNomics: The
National Plan to Empower Black America"

Dr. Claud Anderson is president of PowerNomics Corporation of America, Inc. and The Harvest Institute, Inc. PowerNomics is a company that publishes his books and produces multimedia presentations in which he explains his concept, PowerNomics. PowerNomics is a package of principles and strategies that explain "race" and guide Black America to become a more self-sufficient and economically competitive group in America. Anderson was State Coordinator of Education for Florida under Governor Reubin Askew during the tumultuous 1970s. He led Jimmy Carter's Florida campaign to a win in the state during the presidential election. President Carter appointed Anderson as the federal chairman of a commission of governors of southeastern states. As Assistant Secretary in the U.S. Department of

Commerce, he stimulated and funded economic development projects for the southeastern states. The seafood industry, at that point all wild catch, was a significant sector focus. Dr. Anderson built Maryland's largest seafood-producing facility and operated it for seven years. He owns radio stations, retail food outlets, and a residential construction company. He lectures frequently to business groups, universities, churches, and social organizations on his proposed economic, social, and political solutions.

JAMES ARTHUR BALDWIN
American Novelist, Playwright, Activist

James Baldwin was born in Harlem, New York City. He felt that life in the United States was stifling his creativity, and he went to Europe with the financial assistance of a Rosenwald fellowship. In Europe, Baldwin completed Go Tell It on the Mountain (1953), Notes of a Native Son (1955), and Giovanni's Room (1956). Baldwin became known as the most eloquent literary spokesperson for the civil rights of African Americans and was an ordained preacher. The mid-1960s saw Baldwin's two published plays produced on Broadway, including The Amen Corner, first staged in Washington, D.C. 1955. Baldwin went on to write several more books, essays, and plays. His most outstanding achievement as a writer was his ability to address American race relations from a psychological perspective.

DR. AMOS WILSON
Theoretical Psychologist and Social Theorist

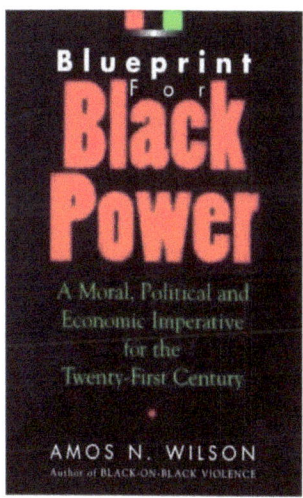

Dr. Wilson was born in 1940 in Hattiesburg, Mississippi. He earned his degrees from Morehouse College, The New School for Social Research, and Fordham University and eventually became a professor of psychology at the City University of New York.

152

A scholar of African studies, Wilson viewed the power imbalances between Africans and non-Africans as a key social issue. He argued that the unique challenges faced by Black people required an educational approach tailored to their needs. He believed that racism, rooted in structural inequalities, could persist without overt expressions and needed societal transformation to be addressed. Wilson lectured globally on the experiences of Black people throughout his career.

DR. JOY DEGRUY
Internationally Renowned Researcher, Educator, Author, Presenter
"Post Traumatic Slave Syndrome: The Study Guide"

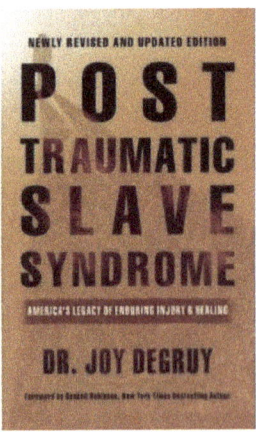

Dr. Joy DeGruy graduated from Portland State University in 1986 with a degree in Speech Communication and earned her Master of Social Work there in 1988. She received her Master of Arts in Clinical Psychology from Pacific University in 1995 and completed her Ph.D. in Social

Work and Social Research at Portland State
University in 2001.

Dr. DeGruy's research examines the links between
racism, trauma, violence, and American chattel
slavery. With over thirty years of experience in
social work, she conducts workshops on
intergenerational trauma, mental health, and social
justice. She authored the influential book "Post
Traumatic Slave Syndrome: America's Legacy of
Enduring Injury & Healing" and created an
assessment scale for measuring respect among
African American male youth.

Dr. MARIMBA ANI
*Anthropologist, African Studies Scholar, Master
Teacher*

Marimba Ani, born Dona Richards, is an accomplished anthropologist and scholar of African Studies. She is renowned for her influential work, Yurugu, which critically analyzes European thought and culture. She is also recognized for coining the term "Maafa," which describes the African holocaust. Ani earned her Bachelor of Arts degree from the University of Chicago and a master's and a Ph.D. in anthropology from the Graduate Faculty of the New School University.

1964, during Freedom Summer, she served as a field secretary for the Student Nonviolent Coordinating Committee (SNCC) and was briefly married to civil rights activist Bob Moses; the couple divorced in 1966. Ani has taught as a Professor of African Studies in the Department of Black and Puerto Rican Studies at Hunter College in New York City, where she played a significant role in introducing the term Maafa to describe the African holocaust.

DR. UMAR JOHNSON
Lecturer, Psychologist, Historian and Author

Dr. Umar Johnson, born Jermaine Shoemake in 1974, is a school psychologist, author, lecturer, and community activist focused on Pan-Africanism. He earned Political Science and Psychology degrees from Millersville University and later obtained a Master of Science in School Psychology and a Doctorate in Clinical Psychology. Johnson worked as a school psychologist in Philadelphia before becoming an assistant principal in Chester, Pennsylvania. He is known for advocating against the mistreatment of Black boys in schools, addressing the school-to-prison pipeline, and educating parents of special education children on ADHD and ADD medications.

BAYYINAH BELLO
Master Teacher, Historian, Humanitarian

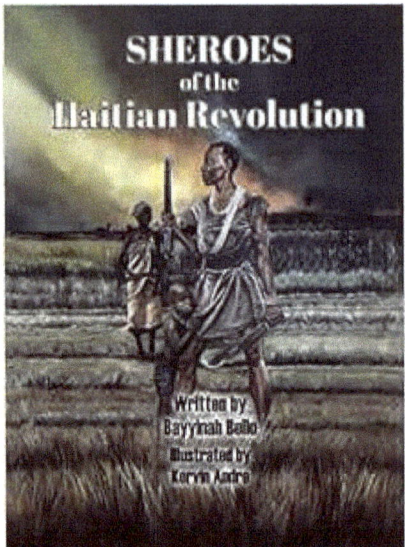

Bayyinah Bello was born in Port-au-Prince, Haiti, and completed her primary education there before joining her father in Liberia. She studied in France and the U.S. and earned a master's degree in linguistics in Nigeria. After returning to the U.S. in 1969, she worked as a publicist and taught French. In 1970, she published her first children's story, "Returning to Haiti," and later founded a bilingual school, Citadel International School.

In 1999, she established Fondation Marie-Claire Heureuse Félicité Bonheur Dessalines (Fondation Félicité) to support the Haitian community. After the 2010 earthquake, she helped launch Friends of Fondation Félicité, a non-profit assisting in Haiti's recovery. Bello was honored at the Gala des Femmes en Flammes in 2014 for her contributions to Haiti. She is a recognized historian and expert on the Haitian Revolution, regularly lecturing and participating in international conferences.

Dr BARBARA SIZEMORE
Educator, Master Teacher, Principal Historian

Barbara Sizemore, born in Chicago in 1927, began her teaching career in the Chicago public school system after earning a bachelor's degree in Classical Languages from Northwestern University. She later received a Master's in Elementary Education in 1954 and a Ph.D. in Educational Administration from the University of Chicago in 1979.

In 1963, Sizemore became one of the first African American women to serve as a principal in Chicago. In 1972, she made history as the first African American woman elected as a superintendent of a major city's school system, overseeing the District of Columbia's public schools for two years.

At the University of Pittsburgh, Sizemore studied schools in low-income, high-crime areas and developed the School Achievement Structure (SAS) educational strategy, which she promoted as dean of DePaul University's School of Education from 1992 to 1998. Sizemore remains active in initiatives to empower students and has received various awards for her contributions to educational theory.

ANTHONY "TONY" BROWDER
Publisher, Cultural Historian, Egyptologist, Artist, Educational Consultant, Author

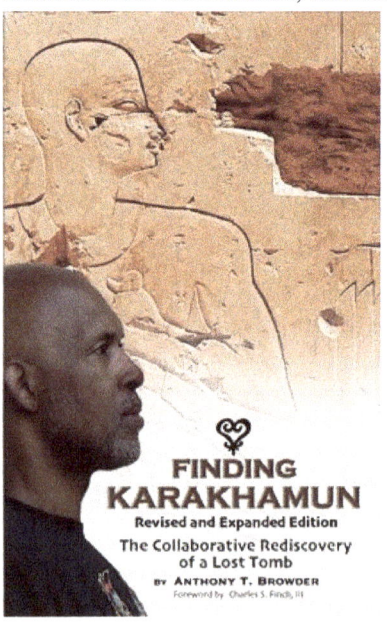

Anthony Browder is a cultural memory specialist, artist, and educational consultant who seeks to challenge distorted perceptions of Africa in media and education. A Howard University's College of Fine Arts graduate, he has lectured globally on African and African American history and culture. As the founder and director of IKG Cultural Resources, Browder has spent 30 years researching ancient Egyptian history, science, and philosophy. He has traveled to Egypt 54 times since 1980 and is currently leading the ASA Restoration Project, which funds the excavation of the 25th dynasty tomb of Karakhamun in Luxor. Browder is the first African American to fund and coordinate an archaeological dig in Egypt, having conducted over 20 missions there since 2009. His research supports the idea that ancient Africans were foundational to civilization and the development of scientific, religious, and philosophical thought. His publications are used in classrooms worldwide.

CARTER G. WOODSON
"Father of Black History," Author

The Mis-Education of The Negro

Originally Published in 1933

By Carter G. Woodson

Carter Godwin Woodson was born in 1875 in New Canton, Virginia. He began high school in his late teens and proved to be an excellent student, completing a four-year course of study in less than two years. In 1915, Woodson helped found the Association for the Study of Negro Life and History (later named the Association for the Study of African American Life and History), which had the goal of bringing African American historical contributions into the public eye.

Woodson was the second African American to receive a doctorate from Harvard, after W.E.B. Du Bois. Known as the "Father of Black History," Woodson dedicated his career to the field of African American history. Woodson lobbied schools and organizations to participate in a unique program to encourage the study of African American history, which began in February 1926 with Negro History

Week. The program was later expanded and renamed Black History Month. He also wrote many historical works, including the 1933 book, *The Miseducation of the Negro.*

PATRICE ÉMERY LUMUMBA
African Nationalist and Pan Africanist

Patrice Lumumba, born in 1925 in Belgian Congo, rose from postal clerk to founder of the country's first nationwide political party, the Congolese National Movement. After leading Congo to independence and becoming its first elected leader in 1960, his rule was cut tragically short. In 1961, he was executed with Belgium's backing, his body subjected to a gruesome disposal - repeatedly buried, exhumed, and ultimately dissolved in acid. For decades, all that remained was a gold-crowned tooth, kept by Belgian police commissioner Gerard Soete who oversaw the destruction. This tooth was finally returned to Lumumba's family in Brussels, a small remnant of a leader who helped shape African independence.

HAILE SELASSIE
Former Emperor of Ethiopia

Haile Selassie I was the 225th and last emperor of Ethiopia, born on July 23, 1892, in a mud hut in Ejersa Goro. Initially named Lij Tafari Makonnen, he was the only legitimate son of Ras Makonnen, governor of Harar. Selassie led a government reflecting his authority, implementing reforms that strengthened education and the police while centralizing his power through a new constitution.

After Italy invaded Ethiopia in 1936, he was exiled but became a symbol of resistance, appealing to the League of Nations for help. With British support, he returned to reclaim the throne in 1941. In the post-World War II era, he aimed to modernize Ethiopia.

He introduced a new constitution in 1955 that promised equal rights for all citizens but did not limit his power. Despite challenges, he remains one of Ethiopia's most popular emperors.

ASHRA and MERIRA KWESI
Historians

For more than 3 decades, Baba Kwesi has served the black community as a historian, interpreter of black cultural heritage, and a leader in Kemetic Spirituality. He was one of the premier students of Dr. Joseph Ben Yochannan. He has led multiple expeditions back to Africa every year for over 30 years. He owns and operates Kemet Nu Productions with his wife, Merira Kwesi. Master Teacher Ashra Kwesi has delivered lectures and guided discussions at Tuskegee, Stanford, and Northwestern University. She has been a featured presenter at the

Pan African Congress in London, Manchester, and Birmingham, England, as well as at the African Holocaust Conference, the Big 12 Black Student Conference, and the National Alliance of Black School Educators.

CHAPTER 7

SPORTS AND ATHLETICS

Athletes of African descent have made remarkable contributions to sports, showcasing immense talent and skill across various disciplines. Their achievements highlight a mix of natural ability, dedication, and hard work, enriching the cultural heritage of sports globally.

Notable historical athletes include:

1. Jackie Robinson (Baseball) - Broke MLB's color barrier in 1947.
2. Althea Gibson (Tennis/Golf) - First Black Grand Slam champion in tennis.
3. Wilma Rudolph (Track and Field) - First American woman with three Olympic gold medals.
4. Flo Jo (Track and Field) - Holds the fastest times in the 100m and 200m events.
5. Willie O'Ree (Hockey) - First Black NHL player in 1958.

Contemporary stars include:

6. Serena Williams (Tennis) - 23 Grand Slam titles.
7. Simone Biles (Gymnastics) - Most decorated gymnast ever.
8. LeBron James (Basketball) - NBA superstar and social advocate.
9. Naomi Osaka (Tennis) - Four-time Grand Slam winner and mental health advocate.
10. Sha'Carri Richardson (Track and Field) - Known for her speed in the 100m and 200m.
11. Bubba Wallace (NASCAR) - Advocates for racial equality in NASCAR.

12. P.K. Subban (Hockey) - Former NHL star and philanthropist.
13. Allyson Felix (Track and Field) - Most decorated American Olympian.
14. Venus Williams (Tennis) - Pioneer for pay equity in sports.
15. Debi Thomas (Figure Skating) - First Black Winter Olympics medalist (1988).
16. Michael Jordan (Basketball) - Widely regarded as one of the greatest basketball players of all time.

THE 1968 OLYMPICS BLACK POWER HUMAN RIGHTS SALUTE

The 1968 Olympics Black Power Salute (human rights salute), a historical moment for history, was an act of protest by the African American athletes Tommie Smith and John Carlos during their medal ceremony at the 1968 Summer Olympics in Mexico City. As they turned to face their flags and hear the American national anthem, they each raised a black-gloved fist and kept it raised until the anthem had finished. Smith, Carlos, and Australian silver medalist Peter Norman wore human rights badges on their jackets.

CHAPTER 8

ARTS, MUSIC & ENTERTAINMENT

All people of the world have a form of music. Music was most likely present before the dispersal of human beings worldwide. Since archaeologists believe that humans originated on the African continent, it is likely that the first music may have been invented in Africa, starting with the basic drum and other influential instruments that were used and then spread and evolved to become an essential part of human life. Continental African and African American music has always influenced and contributed to the world and invented genres that continue to impact the world today.

CLASSICAL MUSIC

JOSEPH BOLOGNE
Afro-French Composer, Violinist & Conductor

Joseph Bologne, Chevalier de Saint-Georges, was a champion fencer, classical composer, virtuoso violinist, and conductor of the leading symphony orchestra in Paris. There has been no documentation found of him as a musician before 1764, when violinist Antonio Lolli composed two concertos, Op. 2, for him, and 1766, when composer François Gossec dedicated a set of six-string trios, Op. 9, to him.

LUDWIG VAN BEETHOVEN
Composer

Ludwig van Beethoven is one of the most beloved composers in history. Often described as a "Mulatto" or "Black Spaniard" due to his mixed heritage—his father was a white German and his mother was of Moorish descent—Beethoven faced significant challenges. He began losing his hearing at age 28 and was completely deaf by his mid-40s. Remarkably, he completed his Ninth Symphony, widely regarded as his masterpiece, in his mid-50s, relying entirely on memory. Beethoven was also a musical innovator, being the first major composer to include a chorus and vocal solos in the final movement of a symphony.

FLORENCE PRICE
Composer

Florence Price was the first African American woman to have her music performed by a major symphony orchestra. On June 15, 1933, the Chicago Symphony Orchestra premiered her Symphony No. 1 in E minor during the concert "The Negro in Music."Marian Anderson regularly performed Price's spiritual arrangement of "My Soul's Been Anchored in the Lord." Price continued to gain recognition in the 1940s and 1950s, and in 1949, she published arrangements dedicated to Anderson. Price passed away in Chicago on June 3, 1953.

SCOTT JOPLIN
Composer, "King of Ragtime"

Scott Joplin was one of the most important and influential composers at the beginning of the 20th century. His groundbreaking ideas around harmony, complex bass patterns, and sporadic syncopation still inspire today's musicians.

SAMUEL COLERIDGE-TAYLOR
Musician

Samuel attended the Royal College of Music as a violin student and received his first commission a year after leaving college.

HAZEL DOROTHY SCOTT
Jazz/Classical Pianist, Singer, Actor
Born in Trinidad, Scott used her fame in the U.S. to improve the representation of black Americans in film.

JAMES WELDON JOHNSON and JOHN ROSAMOND JOHNSON
Poets, Composers of the Black National Anthem
 Initially, "Lift Every Voice and Sing "was written as a poem by James. It was.
Performed for the first time by schoolchildren in celebration of President Lincoln's birthday. The poem was set to music by Johnson's brother, John. It was quickly adopted by the National Association for the Advancement of Colored People (NAACP) as its official song. Today, "Lift Every Voice and Sing" is the most cherished song of the African American Civil Rights Movement and is referred to as the Black National Anthem.

Lyrics to "Lift Every Voice and Sing"

Lift every voice and sing,
Till earth and heaven ring,

Ring with the harmonies of Liberty;
Let our rejoicing rise
High as the listening skies,
Let it resound loud as the rolling sea.

Sing a song full of the faith that the dark past has
taught us,
Sing a song full of the hope that the present has
brought us;
Facing the rising sun of our new day begun,
Let us march on till victory is won.

Stony the road we trod,
Bitter the chastening rod,
Felt in the days when hope unborn had died;
Yet with a steady beat,
Have not our weary feet
Come to the place for which our fathers sighed?

We have come over a way that with tears has been
watered,
We have come, treading our path through the blood
of the slaughtered,
Out from the gloomy past, till now we stand at last
Where the white gleam of our bright star is cast.

God of our weary years,
God of our silent tears,
Thou who hast brought us thus far on the way;

175

Thou who hast by Thy might
Led us into the light,
Keep us forever in the path, we pray.

Lest our feet stray from the places, our God, where
we met Thee,
Lest our hearts, drunk with the wine of the world,
we forget Thee;
Shadowed beneath Thy hand, may we forever stand,
True to our God, true to our native land.

OPERA

CATERINA JARBORO
Opera Singer

Marian Anderson Jarboro was the first African American female opera singer to perform a leading role with an all-white company in the U.S. By 1921, she starred in musicals like "Shuffle Along." In 1930, she debuted in Verdi's "Aida" with the San Carlo Opera Company in Milan and performed as Aida with the Chicago Civic Opera in 1933. She was honored in Wilmington, North Carolina, in 1975, and a star was added to the city's Walk of Fame in 1999.

GRACE BUMBRY
Opera Singer

Grace Bumbry is recognized as one of the leading mezzo-sopranos of her generation. After winning a Metropolitan Opera National Council Audition, she made her concert debut in London and her opera debut in Paris in 1960. From 1960 to 1962, she performed with the Basel Opera, becoming the first Black artist to portray Venus in Wagner's "Tannhäuser." In 1962, she performed at Carnegie

Hall and made her U.S. opera debut at the Chicago Lyric Opera in 1963, earning numerous awards for her contributions throughout the 1960s.

MARIAN ANDERSON
Singer (Classical Music and Spirituals)

Music critic Alan Blyth hailed Marian Anderson's voice as "a rich, vibrant contralto of intrinsic beauty." From 1925 to 1965, she performed with major orchestras in the U.S. and Europe. With church support, she attended music school and made history as the first African American singer at the Metropolitan Opera in 1955.
After studying with B. A. Boghetti, she won a contest to perform at Lewisohn Stadium and debuted at Carnegie Hall in 1928. She toured Europe on a Julius Rosenwald scholarship and sang the national anthem at President John F. Kennedy's inauguration in 1961, later receiving the Presidential Medal of Freedom.

LEONTYNE PRICE
Opera Singer

American soprano Leontyne Price was born in Laurel, Mississippi. She initially studied music before switching to voice and attended The Juilliard School on a full scholarship. Price made her Broadway debut in 1952 and became the first African American leading performer at the Metropolitan Opera in the 1950s and 1960s, debuting there in 1961. She was renowned for her roles in "Il Trovatore," "Antony and Cleopatra," and "Aida." After retiring from opera in 1985, she continued performing recitals until 1997 and returned for a concert honoring September 11 victims in 2001.

PAUL ROBESON
Opera Singer, Actor
Paul Robeson was an American athlete, concert artist, and actor. At 17, he earned a scholarship to Rutgers University and became one of its most decorated students. After a brief law career, he turned to acting and singing during the Harlem Renaissance in the late 1920s, known for roles in The Emperor Jones and Othello. Robeson was also an international activist.

THE BLUES

The blues emerged from various African American songs created by enslaved people, including field hollers, work songs, spirituals, and country string ballads. This rural music authentically captured the suffering and hopes of three hundred years of slavery and tenant farming. Solo musicians typically played the blues on acoustic guitar, piano, or harmonica, performing at parties and juke joints. The original audience was primarily made up of agricultural laborers. The blues significantly influenced the development of jazz and rock music.

Here are a few notable blues artists:
 B.B. King
Muddy Waters
Howlin' Wolf
Etta James
Buddy Guy
John Lee Hooker
Albert King
Koko Taylor
Big Mama Thornton
Freddie King
Black Female Artists:
Etta James
Koko Taylor
Billie Holiday
Ruth Brown
Big Maybelle

JAZZ

Jazz was born in New Orleans, Louisiana, and is fundamentally rooted in the blues. Improvisation is the defining feature of jazz, with musicians often playing sheet music while improvising their solos. Black Jazz musicians invented the modern drum set, and terms like "cool" and "hip" originated within jazz culture. The genre's rich history is closely tied to New Orleans.

Classic Jazz Legends
1. Louis Armstrong – Iconic trumpet player and vocalist who captivated audiences.
2. Duke Ellington – Brilliant pianist and bandleader who transformed jazz into a sophisticated art form.
3. Miles Davis – Groundbreaking trumpet player known for redefining musical boundaries with albums like *Kind of Blue*.
4. Charlie Parker – Genius saxophonist who helped forge the bebop style.
5. John Coltrane – Visionary saxophonist celebrated for deep sound explorations.
6. Ella Fitzgerald – "The First Lady of Song" known for her remarkable vocal talent.

7. Thelonious Monk – Unique pianist whose improvisational style added complexity to jazz.
8. Nina Simone – Powerful voice and activist whose music inspired civil rights movements.

Swing and Big Band Stars
9. Count Basie – Pivotal figure in the swing era, energizing audiences with dynamic performances.
10. Benny Goodman – "King of Swing," known for his clarinet mastery.
11. Billie Holiday – Legendary singer whose deeply moving voice left a lasting legacy.

Modern Innovators
12. Herbie Hancock – A Dynamic pianist whose contributions greatly impacted acoustic and electric

Jazz.
13. Chick Corea – Innovative pianist who shaped fusion and Latin jazz.
14. Wynton Marsalis – Acclaimed trumpet player and dedicated educator.
15. Diana Krall – Smooth stylist known for enchanting performances that bridge classic and modern jazz.

R&B, SOUL, AND FUNK

Soul music is a genre heavily influenced by gospel music, characterized by lyrical and soulful melodies. It strongly emphasizes the rhythm section and often features large horn sections consisting of trumpets, saxophones, and trombones. This genre plays a significant role in the African American community and has evolved into various styles and influenced numerous artists.
Check out this exciting list of standout artists in R&B, soul, and funk!

R&B
1. Mary J. Blige
2. Usher
3. Alicia Keys
4. Toni Braxton
5. Boyz II Men

Soul
1. Aretha Franklin
2. Marvin Gaye
3. Etta James
4. Otis Redding
5. Sam Cooke

Funk
1. James Brown

2. Parliament-Funkadelic
3. Sly and the Family Stone
4. Rick James
5. Earth, Wind & Fire

HIP-HOP AND RAP

On August 11, 1973, DJ Kool Herc, born Clive Campbell, transformed music at a Bronx back-to-school party by pioneering "breakbeat DJing." He isolated and extended instrumental breaks from funk and soul records, energizing dancers and leading to breakdancing. Herc also began rhythmically speaking over these beats, evolving into what we now know as MCing or rapping. This innovation sparked a cultural movement that grew into a global hip-hop phenomenon, significantly impacting music, fashion, and culture while staying rooted in urban American communities.

Here's a short list of notable hip-hop artists:
1. Kendrick Lamar
2. J. Cole
3. Drake
4. Nicki Minaj
5. Jay-Z
6. Kanye West
7. Nas
8. Common
9. The Brat
10. Twista
11. Megan Thee Stallion
12. Missy Elliott

13. Lil Wayne
14. Snoop Dogg
15. Ice Cube
16. Lauryn Hill
17. T.I.
18. Big Sean
19. Future
20. Tyler, The Creator

DRILL AND TRAP MUSIC

Drill music is a subgenre of hip-hop that originated in Chicago in the early 2010s. It shares sonic similarities with trap music and lyrical similarities with gangster rap.

Trap music is another subgenre of hip-hop that originated in Atlanta in the late 1980s and gained worldwide popularity in the 2010s. It is characterized by minimal beats featuring complex hi-hat patterns and tuned 808 kick drums, with lyrical content often focused on gangsta-rap themes and mumbled autotuned vocals.

GOSPEL MUSIC

Enslaved Africans on plantations developed a unique form of gospel music that provided an outlet from their physical captivity. Many songs expressed their complex lives, longing for spiritual and physical freedom, and hope for a better future. One prevalent form of music among Southern Blacks was the spiritual, which uniquely articulated the African American response to oppressive American conditions. Many spirituals contained secret coded messages. For example, songs like "Follow the Drinking Gourd," "Steal Away," and "Wade in the Water" contained instructions for escape. Others, such as "(Sometimes I Feel Like) A Motherless Child" and "I'm Troubled in Mind," conveyed despair felt by enslaved people. The spirituals also served as critiques of slavery, employing biblical metaphors to protest against the enslavement of Black people. This protest can be found in the lyrics of "Go Down, Moses":

Go down, Moses
Way down to Egypt land
Tell ol' Pharaoh
Let my people go.

The spirituals allowed African Americans to transcend their enslaved condition and imagine a life of freedom, as expressed in the song "Ride on, King Jesus, ride on, no man can hinder thee."

A few notable gospel artists: Mahalia Jackson
Thomas A. Dorsey
Andraé Crouch
Shirley Caesar
Kirk Franklin
Yolanda Adams
The Clark Sisters
Richard Smallwood
Tasha Cobbs Leonard
Donnie McClurkin
CeCe Winans
Vickie Winans
Tamela Mann
Le'Andria Johnson

ROCK 'N' ROLL

Rock 'n' roll was born from the black church and nightclubs, heavily influenced by the soul of a remarkable Black woman in the 1940s.
Sister Rosetta Tharpe paved the way for icons like Elvis Presley, Little Richard, and Johnny Cash. Tharpe, now called the godmother of rock 'n' roll, was instrumental in transforming this burgeoning musical style into an international sensation.

Here are a few notable Rock N' Roll artists
Jimi Hendrix
Living Colour
Lenny Kravitz
Prince
Tina Turner
Ernie Isley (The Isley Brothers)
Arthur Lee (of Love)
Gary Clark Jr.
Sly Stone (of Sly and the Family Stone)

Betty Davis
Mavis Staples

REGGAE/DANCEHALL

Reggae derives its name from the term "rege-rege," which means "rags" or "ragged clothes." This provides insight into the origins of reggae music. It began in the late 1960s by Black locals in Jamaica. It was considered a hodgepodge of various musical styles, including Jamaican mento, contemporary Jamaican ska music, and American jazz and rhythm & blues, similar to the music emerging from New Orleans at the time. Many listeners often had difficulty distinguishing reggae from Jamaican dancehall music.

Here are a few notable Dance halls/Reggae:

Petra
Bob Marley
Peter Tosh
Burning Spear
Gregory Isaacs
Jimmy Cliff
Dennis Brown
Toots Hibbert (of Toots and the Maytals)
Buju Banton
Lee "Scratch" Perry
Marcia Griffiths
Black Female Artists:
Rita Marley
Judy Mowatt
Sister Carol
Dawn Penn

HOUSE MUSIC

House music originated in Chicago's club scene in the early 1980s, featuring a steady four-on-the-floor beat at 115-130 BPM. Pioneered by DJs like Frankie Knuckles and Marshall Jefferson, it transformed disco tracks into a more mechanized sound. By 1988, house music gained mainstream popularity and spread to New York and globally, influencing pop artists like Madonna and Lady Gaga while retaining a strong underground presence.

Here are a few notable house music artists from different eras:

Classic House Pioneers:
Frankie Knuckles ("The Godfather of House")
Marshall Jefferson ("Move Your Body")
Larry Heard (aka Mr. Fingers - "Can You Feel It")
Todd Terry ("Weekend")
Adonis ("No Way Back")
Hocus Pocus-Bryan Hadley & Derrick Morris(House it UP)

TECHNO MUSIC

Techno music originated in Detroit in the mid-1980s, thanks to the Belleville Three: Juan Atkins, Derrick May, and Kevin Saunderson. They fused

European electronic influences, like Kraftwerk, with African American styles such as house and funk. The term "techno" became popular in the late 1980s, especially after the 1988 compilation album "Techno! The New Dance Sound of Detroit."

GRUNGE MUSIC

Tina Marie Bell (February 5, 1957- October 10, 2012) was an American singer and songwriter. She was the lead vocalist of the Seattle rock band Bam Bam. She played a key role in pioneering the grunge music movement and is posthumously recognized as "the Godmother of Grunge" and "Queen of Grunge."

TELEVISION and MOVIES

Despite over a century of systemic barriers, Black artists have made significant contributions to television, film, and filmmaking. While many African American entertainers have achieved success and recognition in the face of racism, representation in mainstream entertainment remains disproportionately low. Nevertheless, several prominent Black artists have risen to the highest levels of stardom, demonstrating both the progress made and the continuing need for more significant equity in the industry.

ART and SCULPTURES

The origins of African art exist before what we consider recorded history: sculptures and carvings depicting everyday life have been found all over the continent from ancient Kemet (Egypt) to South Africa and other parts of the world. Famous contemporary black artists include:

Augusta Savage
sculptures

Paul Collins
Artist

Ellis Wilson
Artist

Ernie Barnes
Artist

James C Lewis NOIRE3000
Photography ART

African Art
Tanzania rock art

Fang nglil mask Gabo Africa

Queen Mother Idia 16th century Benin Africa

Copperhead, Ife Yoruba Nigeria

CHAPTER 9

Ballet, Tap, and Choreography

Dancing is often innate among many Black people, showcasing a natural rhythm. African Americans have developed diverse dance styles, with roots tracing back to the traditional dances of enslaved Africans brought to the Americas in the 1500s. These dances merged with European forms, creating a unique blend that preserves African cultural traditions. Dance has played a vital role in African life, allowing enslaved individuals to connect with their homeland and celebrate significant events, such as births and marriages, while enduring hardships.

A few Prominent Black Dancers and
Choreographers**

Ballet:
- Misty Copeland: First African American female
principal dancer at the American Ballet Theatre.
- Arthur Mitchell: First Black principal dancer at
New York City Ballet; founder of the Dance
Theatre of Harlem.
- Alvin Ailey: Innovator of modern dance, blending
ballet.
- Aesha Ash: Former NYC Ballet soloist advocating
for representation.
- Raven Wilkinson: One of the first Black women in
Ballet Russe de Monte Carlo.
- Lauren Anderson: Notable Black principal dancer
at Houston Ballet.
- Carlos Acosta: Cuban dancer with the Royal
Ballet.

Tap Dance:
- Bill "Bojangles" Robinson: Trailblazer in tap
across Broadway and Hollywood.
- Gregory Hines: Renowned master tap dancer.
- Savion Glover: Known for his innovative tap
style.
- Nicholas Brothers (Fayard and Harold): Acrobatic
tap icons in classic films.

- Chloe Arnold: Emmy-nominated choreographer of Syncopated Ladies.
- Brenda Bufalino: Pioneer in blending tap styles.
- Sammy Davis Jr.: Multifaceted entertainer celebrated for tap.

Influential Choreographers:
- Debbie Allen: Acclaimed for theater and education.
- Katherine Dunham: Merged African and Caribbean dance influences.
- Judith Jamison: Former principal dancer and director at Alvin Ailey American Dance Theater.
- Bill T. Jones: Influential modern dance choreographer.
- Pearl Primus: Integrated African traditions into dance.
- Camille A. Brown: Focuses on African American culture.
- Desmond Richardson: Co-founder of Complexions Contemporary Ballet.

These artists have significantly enriched dance, exploring themes of culture and identity.

BREAK DANCING

Break dancing, also known as breaking or B-boying, is a dynamic dance form that emerged in the 1970s among African American and Latino youth in the South Bronx, New York City. This style evolved in major U.S. cities during the 1970s and 1980s, significantly influencing modern dance, especially in rap music videos and performances by artists like Britney Spears. Its mainstream recognition grew in 2004 when break dancers performed for Pope John Paul II at the Vatican, and it was further solidified when the International Olympic Committee included breaking as a sport in the 2024 Olympics in Paris.

CHAPTER 10

MILITARY, REVOLUTIONARIES & WARRIORS

Black Africans have always been warriors, playing crucial roles in wars and leading armies throughout history. Both male and female contributions have often gone unnoticed. From the ancient Kingdom of Kush to the formidable Zulu warriors, their courage and strategic skills have had a profound influence on the outcomes of battles and the destinies of nations. Renowned leaders such as Shaka Zulu and Hannibal Barca exemplified the strength and resilience of black African cultures, leaving a lasting legacy that deserves recognition and respect. Despite facing numerous challenges, these warriors fought not only for their territories but also for the rights and dignity of their people. Here are a few notable warriors to mention.

HANNIBAL BARCA
General, Statesman

Hannibal, general of the Carthaginian army, is considered the most significant military strategist. He lived in the second and third centuries B.C. Born into a Carthaginian military family, he was made to swear hostility toward Rome. Hannibal was known for leading the Carthaginian army and a team of elephants across southern Europe and the Alps Mountains against Rome in the Second Punic War (218–201 BCE).

SHAKA ZULU

Shaka, famously known as a great Zulu king and conqueror, united over a hundred independent Nguni chiefdoms in southeast Africa, between the Drakensberg Mountains and the Indian Ocean, into a lasting Zulu kingdom. Despite later military defeats and efforts to dismantle it, the kingdom endured beyond his death.

Born to Senzangakhona, ruler of a minor Zulu chiefdom, and Nandi, daughter of a Langeni chief, Shaka faced ridicule and bullying in his youth due to his claims of noble descent. However, as he grew, his tall, powerful build and natural leadership emerged, alongside a growing ambition. At around 23, Shaka joined a Mthethwa regiment, where his skills and daring earned him recognition and a sense of fulfillment that set the stage for his rise to power

CETSHWAYO KAMPANDE
The Zulu King

Cetshwayo kaMpande was the king of the Zulu Kingdom from 1873 to 1879 and its leader during the Anglo-Zulu War of 1879. Cetshwayo Kampande was a true hero in a war against the British after the British invaded Zululand, causing the most significant defeat which the English had ever experienced from opposing African leaders.

BEHANZIN HOSSU BOWELLE
West African King

Bowelle ruled during the last years of the 19th century. He was famous for nodding his head whenever he meant the life or death of his subjects. One of his greatest victories was overpowering the 1890 French expedition and making them pay for using the port of Cotonou.

YASUKE
Statesman

Yasuke was a retainer of African origin who served
under the Sengoku Period Japanese daimyō Oda
Nobunaga. Yasuke arrived in Japan in 1579 in the
service of Italian Jesuit missionary Alessandro
Valignano, Visitor of Missions in the Indies, in
India. When Yasuke was presented to Oda
Nobunaga, the Japanese Daimyō thought that his
skin must have been coloured with black ink. When
Nobunaga realized that the African's skin was in
fact black, he took an interest in him. Nobunaga
gave him his own residence and a short, ceremonial
katana. Nobunaga also assigned him the duty of
carrying a weapon. In June 1582, Nobunaga was

attacked and forced to commit seppuku in Honnō-ji in Kyoto by the army of Akechi Mitsuhide. Yasuke was present at the time and assisted in fighting the Akechi forces.

BUFFALO SOLDIERS
Soldiers, U.S. Army

African Americans served in the U.S. Military during the Civil War. Many of these soldiers went on to fight in the Spanish-American War, the Philippine-American War, and continued to serve in the U.S. Army with distinction and honor for the next five decades. With the disbandment of the 27th Cavalry in 1951, the last of the Buffalo Soldiers regiments came to an end.

THE HARLEM HELL FIGHTERS
Soldiers, National Guard

The 369th Infantry Regiment, formerly known as the 15th New York National Guard Regiment. After much debate about whether and how to use African American troops overseas, the 369th would be among the first American regiments to arrive in France, assigned to the French 16th and 161st Divisions. With the French, the Harlem Hellfighters fought at Château-Thierry, Belleau Wood, and many other locations. While several regiment members received commendations for their service, the most lauded men of the 369th are probably Henry Johnson and Needham Roberts. In May

1918, the greatly outnumbered duo fended off a German patrol. Even when wounded and out of ammunition, they fought on and survived to become the first Americans, black or white, to receive the French Croix de Guerre. In 1996, both Roberts and Johnson posthumously received the Purple Heart. A posthumous Medal of Honor was awarded to Johnson in 2015. All told, the 369th spent 191 days in combat, a duration longer than that of any other American unit in World War II.

TUSKEGEE AIRMEN
Soldiers, U.S. Army Air Force

During World War II, Black servicemen of the U.S. Army Air Forces trained at Tuskegee Army Airfield in Alabama, forming the first African American flying unit in the military. Known as the "Tuskegee Airmen," they were part of a program that trained African Americans to fly and maintain combat aircraft.

The Airmen included pilots, navigators, bombardiers, and maintenance staff. They overcame segregation and prejudice, proving that African Americans could effectively operate sophisticated combat planes. Their achievements, along with the support from others, paved the way for the full integration of the U.S. military.

EUGENE JACQUES BULLARD
First African American Fighter Pilot

Bullard was an American expatriate in France when World War I started. He joined the French infantry and received the Croix de Guerre and Médaille Militaire after being wounded. In 1916, he trained as a pilot in the French Air Service and completed 20 combat missions with the Lafayette Flying Corps.

When the U.S. entered the war, Bullard was excluded from the U.S. Air Service because it only accepted white men. After the war, he became a jazz musician in Paris, running a popular nightclub called "L'Escadrille. " He also served as a spy for the French during World War II. Severely wounded again, he left military service and returned to the U.S., living out his days as an unknown hero.

THE ALL-BLACK FEMALE MILITARY
Soldiers, U.S. Army

The 6888th Central Postal Directory Battalion, the only all-female, all-black unit during WWII, the Women's Army Corps (WAC), was tasked with sorting and delivering mail sent to troops stationed throughout Europe. The Six Triple Eights, as they're known, played an instrumental role in boosting soldier morale amid the agonies of war. The battalion had 855 enlisted women and officers and was commanded by Major Charity Edna Adams Early, who became the highest-ranking African American woman in the military at the end of the war. Their battalion's motto was "No mail, no morale." Most of the 6888th worked as postal clerks, cooks, mechanics, and in other support positions. The women worked in three different shifts, seven days a week, processing and delivering mail.

CATHAY WILLIAMS, a.k.a. William Cathay
Soldier, U.S. Army

One of the earliest documented examples of black women serving in combat is the story of Cathay Williams. Born in 1844, Williams who disguised herself as a man, enlisting as "William Cathay" to become a Buffalo Soldier. She served from 1866 to 1868 before a doctor revealed her secret. She was discharged as a Buffalo Soldier and died in 1893.

MARTIN DELANY
Army officer, writer, editor, abolitionist

Martin Delany, U.S. Army officer, writer, editor, abolitionist, Harvard-educated physician, and judge, was the youngest of five children born to a slave father and a free mother. His grandparents, all brought from Africa as slaves, included a Mandingo prince and a village chieftain. Delany was the first African American commissioned as a major in the U.S. Army and a leading anti-slavery activist of the 19th century. A physician and newspaper editor, he founded *The Mystery*, the first African American newspaper west of the Allegheny Mountains.

216

Frederick Douglass later hired him for *The North Star*. Delany believed in self-determination, fighting slavery and segregation while negotiating with West African rulers to establish a black settlement. He explored African repatriation in his treatise *The Origin and Objects of Ancient Freemasonry* and visited Nigeria in the 1850s for land negotiations. Douglass once remarked, "I thank God for making me a man, but Delany thanks Him for making him a black man."

GABRIEL PROSSER
Revolutionary Leader

Born into slavery around 1775, blacksmith by trade and literate, Prosser was described as "a fellow of courage and intellect above his rank in life." He led an unsuccessful slave revolt in Richmond, Virginia, in 1800. His plan was to seize control of Richmond by killing all of the whites except the Methodists, Quakers and Frenchmen, and then establishing a Kingdom of Virginia with himself as monarch. It is estimated that several thousand planned to participate, including many who were to be armed with swords and pikes made from farm tools by slave blacksmiths. Prosser's planned insurrection, for the night of August 30, 1800, was foiled by other slaves who betrayed him and collected rewards for his capture. He was later found guilty and executed.

NAT TURNER
"The prophet"

Enslaved African descendant and Christian preacher who led a rebellion to free himself and other blacks. As a preacher, he traveled from plantation to the plantation ministering to slaves about the word of God. He said God spoke to him and told him to lead a revolt, and to kill his oppressors. He used his preacher network to build his rebellion for freedom. He killed 55 whites before he was caught, tortured, and hanged to death.

DENMARK VESEY
Methodist Preacher, Revolutionary

Vesey was enslaved but freed himself after winning the lottery. He used his platform as a Methodist preacher to recruit supporters for his revolution set for the second Sunday in July of 1822. His plan was revealed by a slave who alerted the white authorities. Hundreds of black slaves were rounded up, including Vesey, who was captured after 2 days. He did not deny the revolt or his plans and was hanged.

A FEW WARRIORS OF THE HAITIAN REVOLUTION

The Haitian Revolution began with a slave revolt in August 1791, led by Jean-Jacques Dessalines. The revolutionaries defeated French forces at the Battle of Vertières in 1803, proclaiming Haiti's independence on January 1, 1804. It was the largest and most successful uprising by self-liberated slaves. Toussaint Louverture initially led the revolt, and by 1792, the rebels controlled a third of the island. Despite heavy casualties—around 100,000 blacks and 24,000 whites—the former slaves repelled French and British forces. By 1801,

Louverture also conquered Santo Domingo, abolished slavery there, and declared himself Governor-General for life over Hispaniola.

Dutty Bookman
Haitian revolution

Dutty Boukman was a self-educated enslaved man from Senegambia, transported to Jamaica and later sold to a French plantation owner in Haiti. He held the position of commander (slave driver) and led secret meetings among enslaved Africans, playing a key role in the Haitian Revolution.

On August 14, 1791, Boukman led a Vodou ceremony at Bois Caïman with priestess Cécile

Fatiman. He delivered an inspiring prayer calling for freedom and resistance against oppression. He emphasized rejecting the white man's god in favor of a just and vengeful deity who would guide them to victory.

Some scholars suggest his nickname, "Book Man," indicates Islamic ties, but he was likely a Zamba, a Vodou spiritual leader. Captured by the French on November 7, 1791, he was beheaded in an effort to suppress the uprising, but his death only fueled the revolution, ultimately leading to Haiti's independence.

Dutty Boukman Prayer:
"The god who created the earth, who created the sun that gives us light. The god who holds up the ocean and makes the thunder roar. Our god who has ears to hear. You who are hidden in the clouds, who watch us from where you are. You see all that the white man has made us suffer. The white man's god asks him to commit crimes. But the god within us wants to do good. Our god, who is so good and so just, orders us to avenge our wrongs. It's He who will guide our efforts and bring us victory. It's He who will assist us. We should all cast aside the image of the white man's god, who is so pitiless. Listen to the voice of liberty that speaks in all our hearts."

Jean-Jacques Dessalines

Haitian revolution
Born 1758, West Africa—died October 17, 1806

He was the emperor of Haiti, who proclaimed his country's independence in 1804.
The Haitian Revolution began with a general slave revolt in August 17911. Inspired by the Declaration of the Rights of Man and of the Citizen, different groups in Haiti sought more freedom. The revolutionaries, led by Jean-Jacques Dessalines, defeated the French forces at the Battle of Vertieres

in 1803 and proclaimed Haiti's independence on January 1, 1804

Sargent Suzanne Belair "The tigress of Haiti"

& Charles Belair,

The Haitian revolution, August 22, 1791-1804

Suzanne Belair, known as Sanite Belair, was one of the female soldiers who fought during the Haitian Revolution. History fails to keep much about her early life. Sanite Belaire is now known as "L'Artibonite," Sanite and her husband, Charles Belair, are responsible for the uprising of almost the entire slave population of L'Artibonite against their masters, The fierce Haitian woman who taught the African warriors of Haiti how to die with dignity after being captured and sentenced to death. Alongside her husband, the executioners tried to blindfold her because she was a woman., Sanite refused. She considered it an insult to be executed any differently than her husband. She watched as her husband was killed., Sanit Belè boldly presented her breast to receive the firing squad's fatal shots. It is said she shouted to the people, "Viv Libète Anba esklavaj!" ("Liberty, no to slavery!").

Cécile Fatima
The Haitian Revolution August 22, 1791, to 1804
1771 - 1883

Cécile Fatiman was a mambo (Vodou high
priestess) who was pivotal in the Haitian
Revolution. In August 1791, she co-led the historic
Bois Caïman ceremony with houngan Dutty
Boukman that sparked the slave uprising in Saint-
Domingue. During this ceremony, Fatiman
sacrificed a black pig in a Petwo rite, and the
attendees drank its blood while swearing an oath to
fight against their French oppressors. She was
reportedly possessed by the lwa Èzili Dantò during
the ritual.

Fatiman proclaimed Boukman as the leader of the rebellion, and the ceremony provided spiritual strength to the revolutionaries. The following uprising led to widespread revolt across Northern Saint-Domingue, ultimately culminating in Haiti's independence in 1804, establishing the world's first Black-led republic. Fatima married Louis Michel Pierrot, who later became a revolutionary army general and Haiti's president.

Marie Saint Dédé Bazile
The Haitian revolution August 22,1791 to 1804

She was a woman who freed herself and did things even some men may have been hesitant to carry out. She had a close relationship with General Janjak Dessalines to supply frontline troops with food, ammunition, And special ops movements. She took up arms in the Haitian Revolution at Bwa Kayiman and fought against the European slavers in Haiti. She also gathered the remains of Jean-Jacques Dessalines and gave him a proper burial after he was beaten and mutilated by his former comrades and left on the Pont Rouge bridge as garbage. She honored the father of the Black Nation. She left us with a legacy of courage.

Victoria Montou
The Haitian revolution August 22, 1791-1804

Adbaraya Toya, known as Victoria Montou, is
originally from the Kingdom of Dahomey, currently
Benin. She was a midwife, a warrior, and a healer.
She trained others in the art of war, including Haiti's
founding father, Jean Jacques Dessalines. Victoria
Montou (known as "Aunt Toya") was a Dahomey
warrior, also called N'Nonmiton, who was captured
and brought to Haiti's sugar plantations. She used
her skills to teach one of the greatest warriors that
ever lived how to fight in hand-to-hand combat and

230

how to throw a knife. Gran Toya guided in Dessalines in his youth, and he called her "aunt." She was an extraordinary warrior, and, as a woman of a certain age, she commanded her indigenous Haitian army after gaining her freedom. In her last battle, she fought off three soldiers and was wounded severely. Before her death, she was able to see Haiti's victory, and she was revered for her bravery and laid to rest as Haiti's mother of independence.

Marie-Jeanneet Lamartiniére
The Haitian revolution August 22,1791 to 1804

MARIE-JEANNE ET LAMARTINIÈRE A LA CRÊTE À PIERROT

She served at the Battle of Crête-à-Pierrot alongside
her husband in 1802 during the Haitian revolution.
She fought in male uniform, bearing both a rifle and
a sword, and was said to use the long rifle to snipe
on the wounded French soldiers below with a skill
all the men admired. Furthermore, she made a great
impression on her fearlessness and courage.
Lamartiniére boosted the morale of her colleagues
with her bravery.

232

CHAPTER 11

MARTIAL ARTS

Martial artists have existed since ancient Africa, with Black people making significant contributions throughout history. Their influence is profound, from traditional fighting styles like Capoeira and Zulu wrestling to modern disciplines such as boxing and mixed martial arts. These martial arts reflect rich cultural histories and philosophies. Many Black martial artists have broken barriers and inspired future generations, showcasing resilience and strength. Their legacies highlight the enduring spirit of martial arts across cultures. Here are a few notable examples:

Tahtib:
A stick-fighting martial art originates in North Africa and dates to the Old Kingdom of ancient Kemet.

Lutte
Traditionnelle (traditional wrestling) is a West African type of fighting that is commonly practiced in Nigeria, Senegal, Niger, Burkina Faso, Togo, and Gambia.

Musangwe:

A South African form of bare fist fighting and boxing.

Nubian Wrestling:

Nuba wrestling is a popular style of wrestling from South Sudan. Nuba wrestling aims to throw rivals to the ground. The Nuba fight has no submissions. Wrestling practiced under the watch of former successful champions. The first portrayal of a Nubian wrestler is on a wall painting from the tomb of Tyanen.

Stunka:
mock fighting that takes place in a festival in
Afgooye, Somalia, on the Somali New Year.

Capoeira

is an African Brazilian martial art that blends dance, acrobatics, and music, developed by enslaved Africans in the early 16th century. Known for its acrobatic maneuvers and fluid movements, capoeira emphasizes the Ginga, a rocking step. The term "capoeira" is believed to come from the Tupi words "ka'a paũ," referring to low vegetation areas where fugitive slaves sought refuge. A practitioner of capoeira is called a capoeirista.

CHAPTER 12

BLACK COWBOYS and BLACK COWGIRLS

Contrary to what you may have been taught in Hollywood and history books, cowboys of color have had a substantial presence on the Western frontier since the 1500s. "Cowboy" is a derogatory term used to describe Black cowhands. Here are a few cowboys and cowgirls to mention:

BRITTON JOHNSON
American Cowboy

Britton was a slave who worked as a foreman on a plantation, enjoying some freedom in his duties. In 1864, during the Elm Creek Raid, his wife and two small children were kidnapped while he was away. Upon his return, he found that his son, Jim, had been murdered, and his wife and remaining children were missing. Johnson spent the summer searching for them in Oklahoma and along the Texas frontier. In the spring of 1865, he lived with the Comanches and arranged a ransom. It's likely his family was rescued in June 1865 by Comanche chief Asa-Havey during peace talks. After reuniting, Johnson moved to Parker County and worked as a freighter.

On January 24, 1871, he and two other Black teamsters were attacked by about twenty-five Kiowa. Reports indicate Johnson fought bravely and died last, defending himself behind his horse.

BILL PICKETT
American Rodeo Cowboy

Bill Pickett developed a strong interest in animals as a child and began working as a ranch hand after fifth grade. He learned cowboy skills such as horseback riding, roping, and cattle herding, quickly excelling in his craft. By 1888, after his family settled near Taylor, Texas, he performed at the town's first fair and co-founded Pickett Bros. Bronco Busters and Rough Riders Association. Although stories vary, Pickett is credited with inventing bulldogging, a technique inspired by how ranch dogs would subdue larger bulls. In one account, a bull's refusal to be herded led Pickett to leap from his horse, bite the bull's lip, and wrestle it into submission. Standing five feet seven inches tall and weighing 145 pounds, Pickett's skill and bravado made him a celebrity in his time. He performed across the U.S., as well as in Canada, Argentina, England, and Mexico. A sculpture of him bulldogging a steer is displayed at Fort Worth Cowboy Coliseum, and he is honored on a postage stamp. Bill Pickett is recognized for introducing bulldogging as a modern rodeo event that involves wrestling a running steer to the ground.

NAT LOVE
"Deadwood Dick"

In 1876, the Gallinger Cowboys (a group Nat belonged to) were sent to deliver a herd of 300 steers to Deadwood, South Dakota. When they arrived, people were preparing for a 4th of July party. One of the organized events was a cowboy contest with a $200 prize to the winner. The contestants competed in roping bridling, saddling, and shooting. Winning every competition hands down, Nat walked away with the $200 prize and the nickname of "Deadwood Dick."

GEORGE FLETCHER
American Cowboy

George Fletcher, a notable Black cowboy, moved
with his family from Missouri to Pendleton, Oregon
around 1900. Growing up near the Umatilla Indian
Reservation, he was adopted by the tribes and
learned their horsemanship skills. Fletcher's rodeo
career began at a local Fourth of July celebration,
leading to his famous appearance at the 1911
Pendleton Round-Up. There, he competed in a
historic Saddle Bronc Finals against Jackson
Sundown, a Native American, and John Spain, a
European American. Though the judges awarded
first place to Spain, the local sheriff and crowd

declared Fletcher the "People's Champion," collecting money to buy him a championship saddle.

DANGERFIELD NEWBY
American Cowboy, Slave Rebellion Participant

Dangerfield Newby was one of several participants in John Brown's raid on the federal arsenal at Harpers Ferry, Virginia in October 1859. Newby became involved in Brown's scheme to facilitate an armed rebellion among the slaves by taking over the arsenal and its surrounding buildings and distributing weapons to enslaved blacks. Newby, who was familiar with the area, supplied arms and other provisions to Brown's brigade. Newby was

246

shot and killed instantly during the gun battle that broke out between white Harper's Ferry townsmen and the rebels.

AMOS HARRIS
American Cowboy, "One of God's True Noblemen"

Amos Harris was a large, tall man who spoke five languages. He was reported to have been born south of Galveston, Texas, on the Brazos River, the son of freed slave parents. He was known as "One of God's True Noblemen." He carried a braided rawhide rope. He was one of the best ropers in the Sandhills.

JOSEPH SEWELL
American Cowboy

Very few African Americans worked as cowboys in nineteenth-century Oregon. One exception was Joseph Sewell, who lived in the Pendleton area. A talented horseman and fighter, Sewell was reportedly killed in a brawl in 1890.

ED HUDDLESTON
"Isom Dart"

Ned Huddleston, also known as Isom Dart, was born into slavery in Arkansas in 1849. At twelve, he followed his Confederate owner into Texas and became a skilled horseman, earning the nicknames "Black Fox" and "Calico Cowboy."

He lived on both sides of the law, rustling horses in Mexico with a bandit named Terresa. After a cattle drive to Brown's Hole in the 1870s and a brief stint in mining, he adopted the name Isom Dart and worked as a bronco buster. Dart returned to Brown's Hole around 1890 to establish a ranch but faced suspicions of rustling cattle. from their ranches. Detective Tom Horn ambushed and killed Isom Dart on October 3, 1900.

JESSE STAHL
American Cowboy

Jesse Stahl was a legendary African American cowboy and rodeo star known for his exceptional bronco riding in the early 1900s. His most famous moment came at the 1912 Salinas Rodeo in California, where he rode the notoriously difficult bronco, Glass Eye, in front of 4,000 spectators. Glass Eye was known for its unique bucking style, but Stahl's performance became a significant part of rodeo history.

Stahl also pioneered "hoolihanding," a daring technique in which he would leap onto a bull's back and wrestle it to the ground, though this practice was later banned. He thrilled audiences with other feats, including "suicide rides" with fellow rider Ty

Stokes. After retiring in 1929, Stahl passed away in Sacramento in 1935.

JOHN WARE
American Cowboy

Ware's strength and remarkable horsemanship earned him a reputation as a cowman who drove as hard as his cattle and whose friends claimed no horse could throw. Eventually settling on his ranch, Ware established himself as one of the most beloved and respected frontier pioneers.

JAMES P. BECKWOURTH
Mountain Man, Explorer

James Beckwourth (1800–1866) was an American mountain man, fur trader, and explorer of mixed African American and European descent. He started as a blacksmith before venturing west to explore the frontier. Known for his fighting skills, he earned the nickname "Bloody Arm."

Beckwourth discovered Beckwourth Pass in California's Sierra Nevada, which became a vital route during the Gold Rush. His autobiography, "The Life and Adventures of James P. Beckwourth," published in 1856, details his experiences as a mediator between Indigenous peoples and settlers. Despite facing racial prejudice, he significantly influenced the history of the

American West before settling in Colorado, where he continued various ventures until his death.

GEORGE GLENN
American Cowboy

George Glenn, an African American trail driver, was born into slavery on March 8, 1850, in Colorado County, Texas. He learned ranching and cooking skills while working on Robert B. Johnson's ranch. After the Civil War, Glenn continued working there.

In spring 1870, he joined Johnson on a cattle drive to Abilene, Kansas. When Johnson fell ill and died in July that year, Glenn had him embalmed and buried in a metal casket. In September 1870, Glenn decided to return Johnson's body to Texas, traveling

253

alone for forty-two days across three states to arrive in Columbus in November 1871. His inspiring story later influenced the TV series Lonesome Dove.

BASS REEVES
Deputy U.S. Marshal

Reeves was an American law enforcement officer. He was the first black deputy U.S. marshal west of the Mississippi River, working mostly in Arkansas and the Oklahoma Territory. Reeves knew the Indian Territory and could speak several Indian languages. As a Deputy U. S. Marshal west of the Mississippi, Reevers served in Indian Territory for 32 years. He killed 14 outlaws and served warrants on over 3,000, including his own son, who was wanted for murder. In 1907, Reeves worked as a patrolman for the police department in Muskogee, where "reportedly no crimes were committed on his beat."

Larry Callies

He was a country singer who lost his voice due to vocal dysphonia. Now, he owns the Black Cowboy Museum in Rosenberg, Texas, which teaches visitors that not everyone in the Old West was white. The Museum houses a collection of artifacts from slaves who journeyed to the Texas Wild West in the 1850s. Callies declares that the first cowboys were Black.

BLACK COWGIRLS

Black women have also played a part in the Old West as cowgirls. Many still ride and compete and win.

Over the years, an all-black rodeo team has been rare, but seeing an all-black female rodeo team has been unheard of until now, thanks to Selina "Pennie" Brown, Sandra "Pinky" Dorsey, Kisha "KB" Bowles, and Brittaney Logan. They met through a veteran horseman, Dr. Ray Charles Lockamy, at a riding event in Maryland. History was made in 2016. More female contestants come to The Bill Picket rodeo each year to compete. Here are a few notable cowgirls to date.

Henrietta "Aunt Rittie" Williams Foster

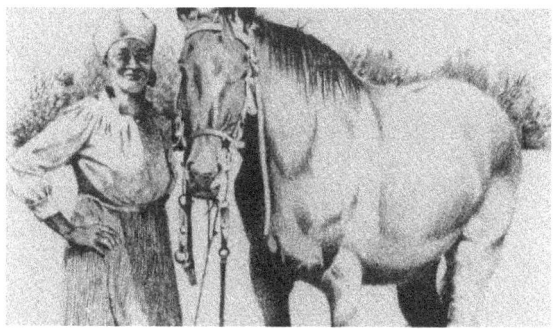

Rittie was born in Mississippi -- the year unknown -- and had five sisters, all sold into slavery. Isaac Newton Mitchell brought her to Texas and purchased her to work on his ranch. She picked cotton, cleaned, cooked, and did laundry for the women. Eventually, Rittie began working cattle and built a reputation for being "tough as any man." She would ride her horse astride in long skirts and could handle the cattle, throw calves, and perform all the same work the men did. An exact date of death can't be found, but she was buried in Refugio and now has a place in the legends of South Texas ranch life.

Johanna July
Born 1857

Johanna July, a black Seminole, was born around 1857 in Nacimiento de Los Negros, the settlement established in northern Mexico following the emigration of Indian and black Seminoles from the Indian Territory in 1849. The July family settled in or near Eagle Pass, Texas, in 1871 when the U.S. Army employed the black Seminoles as translators and scouts because they were familiar with the border country. Johanna learned to tame horses and herd the family's goats and cattle there. With her father's death, she worked the stock and continued to tame wild horses for the U.S. Army and area ranchers. She developed her method of taming horses. She would lead a horse into the Rio Grande, swim up, grab the mane, and gently ease astride. As the horse tired from swimming, they would lose the strength to buck.

Ja'Dayia Kursh
First Rodeo Queen, Arkansas

She faced challenges as the second Black Old Fort Days Dandy in Fort Smith, Arkansas. Despite moments of doubt and backlash after being crowned Miss Rodeo Coal Hill Arkansas, she is now focused on winning Miss Rodeo America and inspiring young girls to pursue their dreams.

"Whenever you see a Black woman on a horse, you can't ignore her," Kursh said. "Being the first Black rodeo queen in Arkansas is bigger than me. It's about the little girls who look up to me. My mission is to empower young women and show them we can be whoever we want."

Here's a list of notable female Black cowgirls, including historical figures and contemporary trailblazers:

Historical Black Cowgirls

1. Mary Fields ("Stagecoach Mary") (1832–1914)
   - One of the first African American women to work as a mail carrier in the U.S.
   - Known for her toughness, she often drove a stagecoach through the rugged terrain of Montana.

2. Bessie Coleman (1892–1926)
   - Best known as the first African American woman pilot, Bessie was also deeply inspired by and associated with the adventurous spirit of the Wild West.

3. Henrietta Williams Foster
   - An accomplished horsewoman and rancher active during the late 19th and early 20th centuries.

Contemporary Black Cowgirls

4. Clemmie Perry
   - Founder of "Women of Color on the Trail," which promotes the legacy and participation of Black women in equestrian sports and trail riding.

5. Kindra Gordon

- An advocate for Black equestrianism, often seen participating in rodeos, parades, and events that celebrate Western culture.

6. Brittany Smart
   - A rodeo competitor and barrel racer who is breaking stereotypes about who can excel in Western sports.

7. Patricia Kelly
   - Founder of Ebony Horsewomen, Inc., a nonprofit organization that empowers urban youth through equestrian training and education.

8. Kimesha Jackson
   - A competitive rodeo rider specializing in barrel racing, helping to increase the visibility of Black women in professional rodeo.

9. Bailey Equestrian
   - A modern-day cowgirl and horse trainer who is passionate about preserving the history of Black cowboys and cowgirls.

10. Nya Campbell
    - A rising star among young Black equestrians, competing in rodeo events and inspiring a new generation.

CHAPTER 13

TRAVEL and DISCOVERY

Not all discoveries were made by Europeans. Many notable explorers, adventurers, and pioneers were Africans or their descendants. Several archaeologists have accounts that prove Africans had already navigated the world before slavery and made their mark on the earth.

Precolonial Evidence

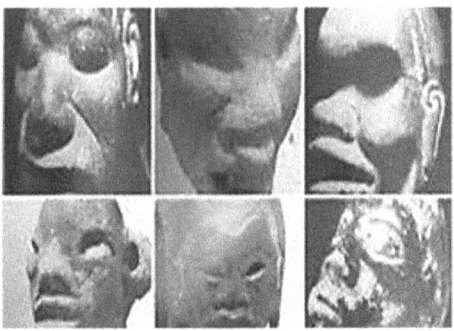

Evidence from ancient Indian stone carvings supports the theory that African (Negroid) people existed in the pre-Columbian Americas. Christopher Columbus first proposed that Black Africans reach the New World before him. In his *Journal of the Second Voyage*, he noted that when he arrived in Haiti (Espanola), the natives described black-skinned people from the south and southeast in ships trading gold-tipped metal spears.

Columbus sent samples of these spears back to Spain for analysis. The alloy composition—18 parts gold, six parts silver, and eight parts copper—matched the metalwork of African Guinea. Columbus's son, Ferdinand, also documented that his father encountered Black people near present-day Honduras.

Other European explorers reported similar findings. In September 1513, Vasco Núñez de Balboa, while descending the slopes of Quarequa (now Panama), encountered several Black men who had been captured. The locals stated that these men lived nearby and were often at war with others. Historian Peter Martyr suggested that these Black men were shipwrecked Africans who had sought refuge in the mountains. Such accounts, corroborated by multiple sources, lend weight to the theory of African presence in the Americas before Columbus.

ABU BAKR II
Emperor of the Mali Empire

SOME IMAGES IN THIS BOOK WERE CREATED BY CANVA AI, CRAIYON AI, AND PIXABAY POWERED BY ISTOCK

Abu Bakr II, also spelled Abubakri and known as Mansa Qu, may have been the ninth Mansa of the

Mali Empire. He was an African emperor who ruled Mali in the 14th century and found the Americas 200 years before Christopher Columbus. He left with 2000 boats and gave up all power and gold to pursue knowledge and discovery. In 1311, he handed the throne over to his brother, Kankou Moussa.

THE MOORS
Astronomers, Artists, Agriculturists and Warriors

SOME IMAGES IN THIS BOOK WERE CREATED BY CANVA AI, CRAIYON AI, AND PIXABAY POWERED BY ISTOCK

The Moors ruled for 700 years in Europe, mainly in what is now Spain and Portugal. They were identified for their presence in Western society, but few people know that the Moors were of African descent, not European. According to the Oxford English Dictionary, moors were described as "all black and indeed swarthy, and hence the term is often used for Negro."

St. Maurice, patron saint of medieval Europe, was only one of many Black officers employed by the Roman Empire. The Moorish advances in mathematics, astronomy, art, and agriculture helped propel Europe out of the Dark Ages and into the Renaissance. They also introduced essential practices like bathing and personal hygiene, which were largely overlooked in medieval Europe. The Moors emphasized the importance of cleanliness, establishing public baths and promoting the use of soap made from olive oil. Their influence contributed to improved public health and hygiene standards that helped transform European society.

JEAN BAPTISTE POINT DU SABLE
"Chicago's First Resident"

Du Sable was born around 1745 in what is now known as Haiti. He began sailing on his father's ships as a seaman, eventually venturing up the Mississippi River to the area now known as Illinois. In the early 1770s, he settled in Peoria, where he gradually acquired more than 800 acres of land. He learned several Indian languages and mastered diplomatic skills, allowing him to form close relationships with the indigenous Potawatomi tribe. In the mid to late 1770s, Du Sable journeyed north. He made his way from the Great Lakes area to the mouth of the present-day Chicago River.

Eschikagou knew this damp, barren, marshy area, variously translated as "Land of the Wild Onions" and "Place of Bad Smells." On the current Tribune Tower site in downtown Chicago, he established the first permanent home in the region. Du Sable created a complex of commercial buildings and a thriving business, capitalizing on the strategic location along the river and lakefront.

MANSA MUSA
Emperor of the Mali Empire

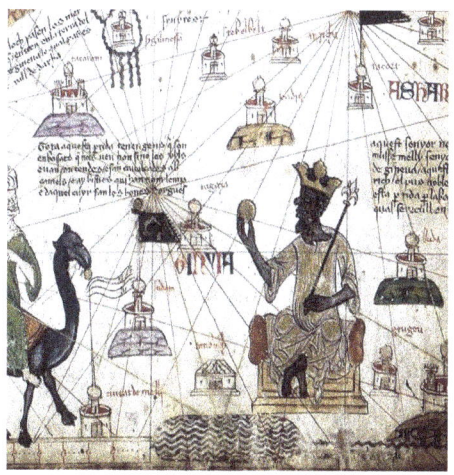

This medieval (14th-century) African ruler made a pilgrimage to the Muslim holy city of Mecca in 1342, which introduced him to the world. Musa began his pilgrimage with an entourage of thousands of escorts and carried considerable amounts of gold, some of which was distributed along the way. Mansa Musa is considered one of the wealthiest individuals in history.

Olmecs
3200 years old

The Olmecs are 3,200-year-old stone heads found in Mexico. They were thought to have traveled from Africa and were called Olmecs. In recent discoveries, Lindquist has found that the ancient Olmecs of Mexico were the Xi People (African Xi), originally from West Africa, and were of the Mende Africans. According to Clyde A. Winters, the Mende script was discovered on many of the ancient Olmec monuments in Mexico and was identical to the same script used by the Mende people of West Africa.

Cheddar Man
9,100 years ago

Cheddar Man is a human male fossil found in Gough's Cave, Cheddar Gorge, Somerset, England. Dating to the Mesolithic period (approximately 9,100 years ago), his skeletal remains suggest he died a violent death. Discovered in 1903, Cheddar Man is one of the oldest nearly complete skeletons of modern humans, Homo sapiens, in Britain. While it was thought humans adapted to lighter skin upon entering Europe around 45,000 years ago for better UV absorption, Cheddar Man's DNA shows markers for pigmentation typically linked to sub-Saharan Africa. This aligns with findings from other Mesolithic remains across Europe.
Source: Natural History Museum
https://www.nhm.ac.uk/discover/cheddar-man-mesolithic-britain-blue-eyed-boy.html – "Cheddar Man: Mesolithic Britain's Blue-Eyed Boy" by Kerry Lotzof.

Sweden Man
7,000 years old

SOME IMAGES IN THIS BOOK WERE CREATED BY CANVA AI, CRAIYON AI
AND PIXABAY POWERED BY ISTOCK

Genetic analysis of a 7,000-year-old hunter-gatherer
skeleton from Spain, La Braña 1, reveals
unexpected traits: dark skin, hair, and blue eyes.
This finding challenges the belief that lighter skin
developed shortly after early Europeans migrated
from Africa around 45,000 years ago. Lead
researcher Dr. Carles Lalueza-Fox suggests that the
evolution of lighter skin may have occurred much
more recently, within the last 7,000 years, reshaping
our understanding of human evolution and
environmental adaptation.

Matthew Henson
African American explorer

Orphaned young, Matthew Henson (1866-1955) began his maritime career at age 12 aboard the *Katie Hinds*, sailing worldwide for six years. At 20, his expertise led explorer Robert E. Peary to recruit him. After six failed Arctic expeditions together, Henson reached the North Pole first on April 6, 1909, planting the American flag 45 minutes before Peary. Though recognition came decades later with a Navy Medal (1945) and other honors, his groundbreaking achievement was finally celebrated with his 1988 reinterment at Arlington National Cemetery beside Peary.

CHAPTER 14

Black Towns and Settlements

One of the first black towns in the United States was founded in 1835 by "Free Frank" McWhorter, a former slave from Kentucky. This short-lived community was known as New Philadelphia, Illinois. In the years following the Civil War, more black towns emerged, created by former slaves seeking to own land and build a community free from interference. Most of these towns developed during the waning years of Reconstruction. Unfortunately, many of these communities did not survive due to hostility from envious white neighbors and pervasive racism. Some towns were burned down, while others were destroyed when highways or expressways were built through them via eminent domain. Additionally, some were deliberately flooded by rivers and lakes as a tactic employed by non-black neighbors. Despite these challenges, black people successfully established towns for themselves.

BLACK WALL STREET
TULSA, OK, GREENWOOD

Founded in 1906, Greenwood emerged on Indian Territory, an area where Native American tribes had been forcibly relocated. Some African Americans, former slaves of these tribes, acquired land through the Dawes Act, while others, fleeing racial oppression after the Civil War, sought a better life in Oklahoma.

Promoted as a safe haven for African Americans, Oklahoma saw a surge in Black townships.

However, on May 31, 1921, an incident involving a young Black man and a young white woman incited a white mob to attack Greenwood. The alleged assault resulted in hundreds of Black residents

276

killed and over 1,000 homes destroyed. Before this tragedy, Greenwood was one of the most prosperous African American communities in the U.S., with a school system, 21 restaurants, one hospital, six private planes, and over 600 businesses.

SENECA VILLAGE
LOWER MANHATTAN, NEW YORK CITY

Seneca Village was a self-contained African American community from 1825 to 1857. In 1825, John and Elizabeth Whitehead began selling their farmland, with Andrew Williams purchasing the first three lots for $125. The community grew as

277

members of the African Methodist Episcopal Zion Church, the most prominent Black church in the country, bought plots. By 1855, the population reached about 225, primarily African American. Seneca Village included around 50 homes, three churches, and a school, with a local spring providing fresh water. Residents also had gardens and livestock. Unfortunately, the city displaced this thriving community to build Central Park, which occupied the area between West 82nd and West 89th Streets and 7th and 8th Avenues. Notably, Black residents owned land in Seneca Village even while slavery remained legal in the South.

THE HAYTI COMMUNITY, DURHAM, N.C.

After the Civil War, freedmen in Durham, N.C., began settling on the southern edge of the city. Key figures in the community, James E. Shepard, Aaron McDuffie Moore, John Merrick, and Charles Clinton Spaulding, named the area Hayti, inspired by Haiti, the first free Black republic in the Western Hemisphere.
They established the North Carolina Mutual Life Insurance Company, which became the wealthiest Black-owned company of its time, and a land-development company that built homes and businesses in the region.
By the early 1900s, Hayti had become a self-sufficient Black community, featuring Lincoln Hospital, a theater, a library, hotels, and over 200

279

businesses. North Carolina Central University, founded in Hayti in 1910, became the first state-funded liberal arts HBCU in 1925. However, the community began to decline due to urban renewal efforts that divided it with a freeway.

JACKSON WARD, RICHMOND, VA.

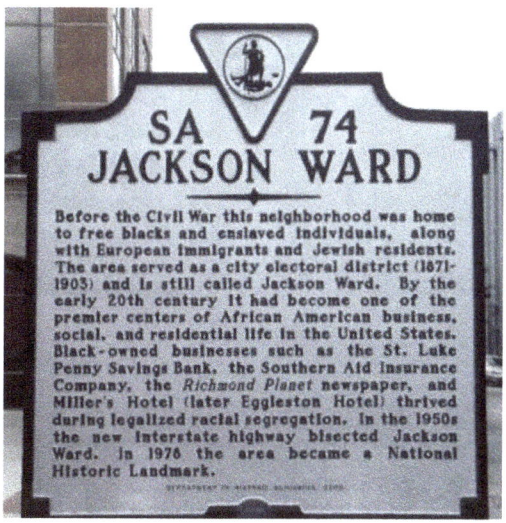

Virginia's Capitol is in Jackson Ward, a Richmond neighborhood historically significant to the black community. After the Civil War, newly freed slaves settled here, leading to a thriving business sector known as the "birthplace of black capitalism" and the "Harlem of the South." A key figure, Maggie L.

Walker, founded the St. Luke Penny Savings Bank in 1910, becoming the first black woman to establish a bank in the U.S.

Unfortunately, the all-white City Council targeted Jackson Ward for revitalization, resulting in a federal housing project that displaced many families. Ultimately, the Virginia State Assembly's decision to route Interstate 95 through the neighborhood further decimated this historic community.

BRUCES BEACH
MANHATTAN BEACH, CALIFORNIA

Willa and Charles Bruce purchased the land for $1,225 in 1912, and it is now worth approximately $6 million. The property, located at the bottom of a hill just a few blocks from the beach between 26th and 27th Streets, featured rolling grassy terraces with benches and trees. It served as a resort run for and by Black residents. However, the couple faced increasing harassment and threats from their white neighbors and the Ku Klux Klan. The KKK even set fire to a central deck, and Black visitors were forced to walk half a mile to reach the beach due to roadblocks that were established. Despite this violence and intimidation, the Bruces' enterprise endured, providing rare beach access to African Americans in California. In 192 4, city officials condemned the neighborhood and seized the property, claiming it was needed for a park, although this park was never created. The land changed ownership multiple times and remained vacant for decades. In 2021, the LA County began issuing apologies for the seizure. After 96 years, the descendants of Willa and Charles Bruce will finally regain ownership of Bruce's Beach.

Oak Bluffs on Martha's Vineyard
"The Inkwell"

The Inkwell, or Town Beach in Oak Bluffs,
Massachusetts, part of Cape Cod's historic African
American summer resorts since the 1890s, was
named pejoratively by nearby whites referencing
the skin color of its beachgoers. Initially attracting
African Americans as servants for white summer
residents, some early Black workers later became
property owners and entrepreneurs despite racial
discrimination. Women played a pivotal role in the
community's growth, offering accommodations in
their cottages for Black visitors. Shearer Cottage,
founded in 1912 by Charles and Henrietta Shearer,
began as Henrietta's laundry in 1903 and remains
family-run today. From the 1950s to the early
1970s, middle-class Black families purchased
affordable cottages, many rising significantly in

value. By 2010, Oak Bluffs had become one of the wealthiest Black resort communities, known for attracting famous visitors.

Lake Lanier was known as Oscar Ville, Forsyth County, Georgia.

Oscar Ville was a thriving Black community of carpenters, blacksmiths, and bricklayers, with farming as the primary trade. In 1912, after the death of Mae Crow, a 19-year-old white woman, violent mobs called "night riders" terrorized Oscar Ville, driving out its Black residents. Fires and firebombs destroyed the church, the heart of the community, where many sought refuge. In the late 1950s, Buford Dam was built, creating Lake Lanier, which submerged Oscar Ville's history. Many believe the lake is haunted due to frequent drownings, as the flooded town, including tall trees and structures, creates dangerous underwater hazards.

CHAPTER 15

African Empires

Before colonization, many African empires existed throughout the continent. These empires were rich in minerals and natural resources and were significant trade centers. Each empire had its tribes, nations, and political and spiritual systems. Africa is still the primary source of the world's progress.

Mali Empire

Timbuktu, founded around 1100 CE in Mali, became a vital trade center during the Mali Empire from the 13th to 15th centuries. Its strategic location near the Niger River facilitated connections between central Africa and North Africa, leading to wealth from trade in commodities like gold, salt, ivory, and slaves. At its peak in the mid-15th century, Timbuktu had around 100,000 inhabitants, with trade often conducted through barter or valuable items like gold ingots and cowry shells.

Under Mansa Musa's reign in the 14th century, Timbuktu flourished as a center of Islamic learning, housing several universities and extensive libraries that taught subjects such as theology, medicine, and astronomy. The city's name comes from the Tuareg language, with interpretations ranging from "place of Buktu" to "the place between dunes." Archaeological evidence indicates that the area has been significant since the Neolithic period, with early settlements and trade in copper and gold contributing to its economic importance.

Kingdom of Kongo
1390 – 1914

The Kingdom of Kongo was prominent in the western part of central Africa. The name comes from the fact that the kingdom's founders were Kikongo-speaking people, and the spelling of Congo with a C comes from the Portuguese translation. Kingdom was founded around 1390 CE through the political marriage of Nima a Nzima, of the Mpemba Kasi, and Luqueni Luansanze, of the Mbata, cemented the alliance between the two Kikongo-speaking peoples. The Kingdom would reach its peak in the mid-1600s. The Kingdom of Kongo eventually fell to scheming nobles, feuding royal factions, and the Trans-Atlantic slave trade,

289

initiating its eventual decline. The Kingdom was centered around the great city of Mbanza Kongo, located in what is now northern Angola, (location: 6°16′04″S 14°14′53″E), which was later renamed to São Salvador. In 1888, what was left of the Kingdom of Kongo was made a vassal state to Portugal, and in the early 1900s it was formally integrated into the Portuguese colony in Angola. The Kingdom of Kongo was a 'commonwealth' rather than a Kingdom, as they were built, in part, on mutual agreement, marriage alliances, and cooperation rather than conquest.

Kingdom of Aksum
100–940 AD

Axumite currency

The Kingdom of Aksum or Axum, also known as the Aksumite Empire and Abyssinia, was an important trading nation in northeastern Africa, existing from approximately 100–940 AD. It grew from the proto-Aksumite Iron Age period ca. 4th century BC to achieve prominence by the 1st century AD and was a major player in the commerce between the Roman Empire and Ancient India. The Aksumite rulers facilitated trade by minting their own currency, the state established its hegemony over the declining Kingdom of Kush and regularly entered the politics of the kingdoms on the Arabian Peninsula, eventually extending its rule over the region with the conquest of the Himyarite Kingdom. Under Ezana (fl 320–360), Aksum became the first major empire to convert to Christianity and was named by Mani (216–276) as one of the four great powers of his time, along with Persia, Rome, and China. In the 7th century the Muslims, who originated in Mecca, sought refuge from Quraysh persecution by traveling to Aksum (Abyssinia), a journey famous in Islamic history as the First Hijra. Aksum's ancient capital is found in northern Ethiopia. The Kingdom used the name "Ethiopia" as early as the 4th century. It is also the alleged resting place of the Ark of the Covenant and the purported home of the Queen of Sheba.

Ancient Empire of Ashanti
17th century

The Ashanti Empire rose in 17th-century West Africa (modern Ghana) from small Akan chiefdoms centered around Kumasi, gaining prominence through trade with the Portuguese for gold.

Osei Tutu (1701-1717), the Asantehene, united the chiefdoms into a centralized state, established Kumasi as the capital, created a constitution, and founded the Odwira festival. He introduced the Golden Stool as a sacred symbol of Ashanti authority, legitimizing his and future rulers' power. The empire's wealth centered on gold, used as currency in gold dust.

The Zulu Kingdom

sometimes referred to as the Zulu Empire or the Kingdom of Zululand, was a monarchy in Southern Africa that extended along the coast of the Indian Ocean from the Tugela River in the south to Pongola River in the north.

The kingdom grew to dominate much of what is today KwaZulu-Natal and Southern Africa. In 1879, the British Empire invaded, beginning the Anglo-Zulu War. After an initial Zulu victory at the Battle of Isandlwana in January, the British Army regrouped and defeated the Zulus in July during the Battle of Ulundi. The area was absorbed into the Colony of Natal and later became part of the Union of South Africa.

Oyo empire
17th to 19th century CE

The Oyo Empire emerged in what is now the southwest

Nigeria, becoming a dominant force among Yoruba societies. With its capital at Old Oyo near the Niger River, the empire grew wealthy through trade, particularly in the trans-Atlantic slave trade, leading to the region's designation as the 'Slave Coast'. The Oyo traced their origins to the Kingdom of Ife (11th-15th centuries CE).

From 1450 CE, trade with European powers – initially led by the Portuguese, followed by the British, French, and Dutch – brought prosperity. The empire traded local goods including palm oil, kola nuts, pepper, and ivory, while also maintaining a significant iron-working industry. However, pressure from northern Islamic states led to the empire's collapse by the mid-19th century, resulting in its fragmentation into rival chiefdoms. This fragmentation left local populations vulnerable to enslavement until the 1850s CE.

The region later became part of British colonial Nigeria, which unified in 1914 CE and achieved independence in 1960 CE.

Kingdom of Zimbabwe
(1220-1450 AD)

The word Zimbabwe loosely translates to "House of Rock," derived from the Shona terms dzimba dza mabwe (great stone houses) or dzimba woye (esteemed houses). The Shona people, original inhabitants of the Zimbabwe plateau, developed a structured society over centuries, eventually forming the Kingdom of Zimbabwe with its capital at Great Zimbabwe. Renowned stonemasons and traders specialized in ivory and gold, which drove their economy. Their ancient stonework and artifacts still stand today.

The Kingdom of Kush
(ca. 2686 B.C. – 1650 BC)

Kush existed during Egypt's Old and Middle
Kingdoms, centered around Kerma in Upper Nubia
near the Third Cataract of the Nile. It rose to power
during the Second Intermediate Period, based at
Napata in modern Sudan. As Lower Egypt fell to
the Hyksos, Kush became dominant in Upper
Egypt. Still, he was soon defeated when the 18th
Dynasty expelled the Hyksos and turned south,
making Nubia an Egyptian colony under a Viceroy
of Kush. Egypt's control weakened after the New
Kingdom's collapse (ca. 1070 BC), allowing local

leaders to regain power. Kush was renowned for its skilled archers, earning the nickname "Land of the Bow."

Pre-Human Migration Out of African Map

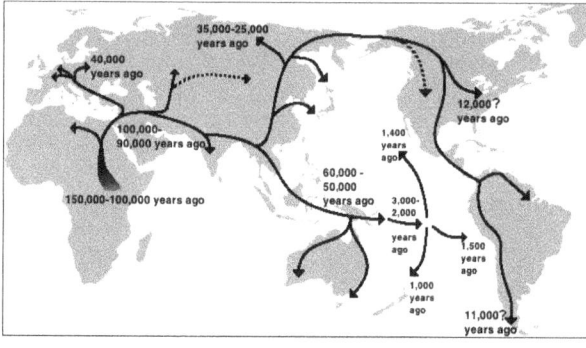

Pre-colonial map of Africa And Map of Ancient Africa

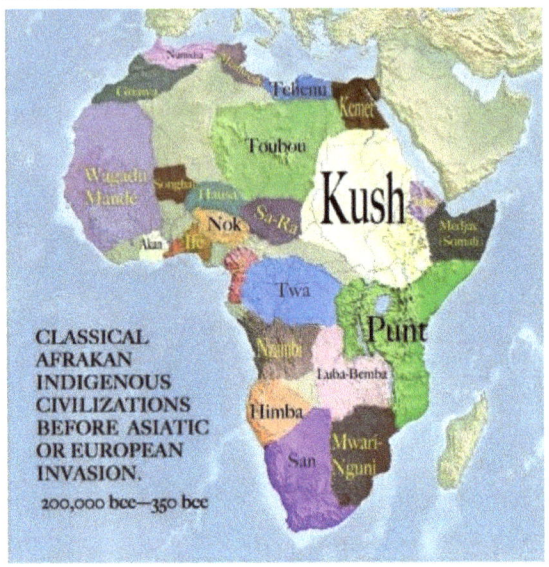

Maps of the route of the slave transatlantic trade

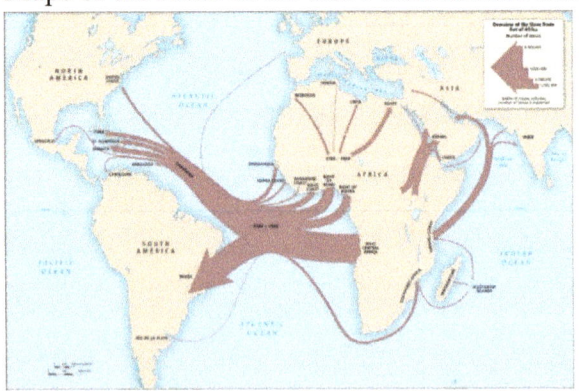

https://www.slavevoyages.org/blog/all-intro-maps

CHAPTER 16

OTHER BLACK FACTS and CONTRIBUTIONS

Black people have significantly contributed to the world in various fields, including inventions, architecture, and beyond. There have been so many contributions that mentioning them all in one book would be impossible. Moreover, Black individuals continue to make impactful contributions every day. Here are a few more noteworthy examples to consider:

Foods Native to Africa

- Rice
- Yams
- Coffee
- Black eye peas
- Okra
- Watermelon

Black people were lynched in America for a variety of racist and oppressive reasons, primarily to enforce white supremacy and racial control.

The main reasons included:

1. Perceived Threat to White Supremacy – Many lynchings were carried out to terrorize Black communities and maintain white dominance, especially in the South after Reconstruction.

2. Economic Competition – Black people who became successful business owners, landowners, or labor competitors were often targeted to prevent economic advancement.

3. Accusations of Crimes Against White People – False or exaggerated accusations, particularly against Black men, were common justifications for lynchings. This included claims of theft, assault of a white woman, disrespect toward and even looking at any white person, even if it were a child.

4. Alleged Sexual Relations with White Women (white women lying)– One of the most frequent justifications for lynchings was the accusation that a Black man had raped or had consensual relationships with a white woman. The mere suggestion of such an interaction could lead to violent retaliation.

5. Violating Social Norms (Jim Crow Etiquette) – Black people were lynched for actions perceived as "stepping out of their place," such as speaking out against racism, voting, refusing to move off sidewalks for white people, or not addressing white individuals with expected deference.

THE BLACK TRUTH ABOUT HISTORY FROM PAST TO PRESENT

6. Political Activism & Civil Rights Efforts
– Black people who registered to vote, ran
for office, organized communities, or
challenged segregation laws were often
targeted to prevent political and social
progress.

7. Mob Violence and Entertainment – Some
lynchings were public spectacles, where
white crowds, including families, gathered
to watch, take photos, and celebrate the
brutalization of Black individuals as a form
of racial terrorism.

Terms and Definitions you should know-

AAVE (African American Vernacular English)
– A dialect of English commonly spoken by
many African Americans, with its distinct
grammar, vocabulary, and pronunciation
patterns. It has roots in West African languages
and Southern English dialects and is an essential
part of Black culture and identity.

Meritorious Manumission – A legal practice in
which enslaved individuals could be granted

freedom as a reward for acts that benefited their enslavers or society, such as saving a white person's life, inventing something useful, or betraying a fellow enslaved person.

Black Codes – Laws enacted in the Southern United States after the Civil War (1865–1866) that restricted the freedom of Black people, limiting their rights to own property, work in specific jobs, and move freely. These laws were designed to maintain racial hierarchy and control the labor force.

Redlining – A discriminatory practice in which banks, insurance companies, and other financial institutions systematically denied loans or services to Black individuals and communities, often based on racially biased maps. This practice contributed to racial wealth disparities and housing segregation.

Jim Crow – A system of laws and customs in the United States (late 19th century to mid-20th century) that enforced racial segregation and discrimination against Black people, particularly in the South. It institutionalized racial oppression in public spaces, education, employment, and voting.

Self-Hate – A psychological condition in which individuals internalize negative societal beliefs about their own racial or cultural group, leading to feelings of inferiority, rejection of their heritage, or preference for dominant cultural norms.

Stockholm Syndrome – A psychological response in which captives develop feelings of trust, affection, or dependence toward their captors as a survival mechanism. This concept has been used to analyze the ways some enslaved or oppressed individuals adapted to their conditions.

Enslaved – A person who is forcibly held in bondage and denied basic human rights, often forced to work without pay under threat of violence or death. The term "enslaved" is preferred over "slave" because it acknowledges the humanity of the person rather than defining them solely by their condition.

Indentured Servitude – A labor system in which individuals agreed to work for a set number of years in exchange for passage to a new country, room and board, or other benefits. Unlike slavery, indentured servitude had an endpoint, but conditions were often harsh, and some indentured servants faced brutal treatment.

Black Culture – The customs, traditions, language, art, music, literature, and social practices developed and passed down within Black communities, particularly those of African descent. It is deeply rooted in African heritage, shaped by historical experiences such as enslavement and civil rights struggles, and continues to influence global culture today.

Juneteenth – A federal holiday in the United States, observed on June 19th, commemorates enslaved African Americans' emancipation. It marks the day in 1865 when Union troops arrived in Galveston, Texas, and announced that enslaved people were free—more than two years after the Emancipation Proclamation.

Hotep is a term from the ancient Egyptian (Kemet) language meaning "peace" or "satisfaction." It is sometimes associated with Afrocentric ideology and Black empowerment in modern usage. However, it has also been used pejoratively to describe individuals who promote misogynistic, homophobic, or pseudo-intellectual views under the guise of Black consciousness.

Melanin is a natural pigment found in the skin, hair, and eyes that helps protect against UV radiation. Individuals with darker skin have higher levels of melanin, which not only influences skin tone but is also celebrated within Black communities as a symbol of beauty and resilience. For the past 60 years, melanin has been the subject of various studies.
Additionally, melanin can affect movement, and dance can help absorb sunlight.

Cognitive Dissonance –
Psychological discomfort is experienced when a person holds conflicting beliefs, values, or attitudes. In the context of race and history, this can explain how people justify oppressive systems or struggle to reconcile historical truths with personal or societal beliefs.

Post-Traumatic Slave Syndrome (PTSS)– A concept developed by Dr. Joy DeGruy that describes the multigenerational trauma experienced by descendants of enslaved Africans. It explains how the legacy of slavery, racism, and systemic oppression continues to impact Black individuals and communities through behavioral patterns, stress responses, and social structures.

Sambo – A historically racist stereotype depicting Black men as docile, lazy, and unintelligent, often used in literature, minstrel shows, and media to justify racial oppression. The term has deep roots in anti-Black racism and was used to reinforce the idea that Black people were content with enslavement or subjugation.

Coon – A derogatory slur and racist caricature that portrays Black individuals, especially men, as foolish, submissive, or eager to entertain white audiences. The "coon" stereotype was popularized in minstrel shows and used to mock Black speech, behavior, and intelligence.

Bedwench – A derogatory term used to describe a Black woman who is perceived as being submissive to, or in relationships with, white men, particularly for personal gain or social status. Historically, it references the sexual exploitation of Black women during slavery but is now often misused to police Black women's choices.

Nigger – A highly offensive racial slur with a history of being used to dehumanize and oppress Black people. It originated from the Latin word *niger* (meaning "black") but became a term of racial hatred, particularly in the U.S. during slavery and segregation. In some Black communities, a reappropriated version (*nigga*) is used as a term of camaraderie, though it remains controversial.

Casual Killing Act:
Passed in 1669 in colonial Virginia, the Casual Killing Act legalized the killing of an enslaved African by a white person without serious punishment, as long as the act occurred during the "correction" of the enslaved individual. This law reinforced the brutal control of slavery by dehumanizing Black people and shielding slaveholders from consequences. Often, it also served to protect the slave master's wife from being arrested for such actions.

Reckless Eyeballing:
Reckless eyeballing was a term used, especially in the Jim Crow South, to describe a Black man allegedly looking at a white woman in a way considered inappropriate. It was a racist accusation that could lead to severe punishment, including lynching, even without any real wrongdoing. It reflects the deep racial injustice and social control during segregation.

Montgomery Bus Boycott:

The Montgomery Bus Boycott (1955–1956) was a political and social protest against racial segregation on public buses in Montgomery, Alabama. It began after Rosa Parks was arrested for refusing to give up her seat to a white person. The boycott lasted over a year and was a major catalyst for the Civil Rights Movement, helping to bring Dr. Martin Luther King Jr. to national prominence.

Slave Breeding:
Slave breeding refers to the forced reproduction of enslaved Black people in the United States to increase the slave population, especially after the transatlantic slave trade was banned in 1808. Enslaved men and women were treated as property, and owners would manipulate or coerce them to have children, treating human beings as commodities.

The Last Slave Ship:
The last known slave ship to bring enslaved Africans to the U.S. was the Clotilda in 1860, decades after the international slave trade was outlawed. It illegally transported African captives to Alabama. Some of the survivors later founded Africatown near Mobile, Alabama. The wreckage of the Clotilda was discovered in 2019.

14th Amendment:
The 14th Amendment to the United States Constitution was ratified in 1868 during the Reconstruction Era. It grants citizenship to "all persons born or naturalized in the United States," including formerly enslaved people, and guarantees equal protection under the law. It has been a critical tool in civil rights cases throughout American history.

FLAG, SIGNS, AND SYMBOLS

UNIA flag
The UNIA meaning of the colors of the flag: red is
the color of the blood which men must shed for
their redemption and liberty; black is the color of
the noble and distinguished race to which we
belong; green is the color of the luxuriant vegetation
of our Motherland. Red, black, and green

The Black American Heritage Flag
was created by Melvin Charles and Gleason T.
Jackson in Newark, New Jersey, inspired by their
feelings of underrepresentation in parades as
children.
The flag features a gold-blunted sword symbolizing
pride, a fig wreath representing peace and

prosperity, red for the bloodshed of Black people, and black for pride in melanin.

Adinkra Symbols

Adinkra are visual symbols from the Gyaman people of Ghana and Côte d'Ivoire. Used initially as royal cloth prints, they extend beyond their origins, appearing on logos, clothing, and architecture. These symbols represent Akan and African cultural concepts, often accompanied by traditional proverbs.

Popular African Adinkra Symbols

MORE INVENTORS AND THEIR INVENTIONS

Shoe Lasting Machine Jan Matzeliger
Ironing Board Sarah Boone
Lubricators   Elijah McCoy
Horse Bridle Bit L.F.Brown
Rocket Catapult Hugh MacDonald
Horse shoe   Oscar E. Brown
Elevator   Alexander Miles
Pacemaker   Otis Boykin
Gas Mask   Garrett Morgan
Guide Missile Otis Boykin
Traffic Signal Garrett Morgan
Lawn Mower   John A. Burr
Hair Brush   Lyda Newman
Typewriter   Burridge & Marshman
Heating Furnace   Alice H. Paker
Train Alarm   R.A. Butler
Airship   J.F.Pickering
Radiation Detector   Geo. Carruthers
Folding Chair Purdgy/Sadgwar
Peanut Butter George W. Carver
Hand Stamp   W.B. Purvis
Paints & Satins   George W. Carver
Fountain Pen W.B. Purvis
Lotion & Soaps George W. Carver
Dust Pan L.P.Ray
Automatic Fishing Reel George Cook
Insect Destroyer Gun A.C. Richardson
Ice cream Mold A.L. Cralle
Baby Buggy   W.H. Richardson
Blood Plasma Dr. Charles Drew
Sugar Refinement N. Rillieux
Horse Riding Saddle Wm. D. Davis
Clothes Dryer G.T. Sampson
Shoe   W.A. Detiz
Celluar Phone Henry Sampson
Player Piano Joseph Dickinson
Pressing Comb Walter Sammons

Arm for Recording Player Joseph Dickinson
Curtain Rod S.R. Scottron
Doorstop O. Dorsey
Lawn Sprinkler J.W. Smith

Automatic Gearshift R.B. Spikes
Photo Print Wash Clatonia J. Dorticus
Urinalysis Machine Dewey Sanderson
Photo Embossing Machine Clatonia J. Dorticus
Hydraulic Shock Absorber Ralph Sanderson
Postal Letter Box P.B. Dowing
Refrigerator J. Standard
Toilet T. Elkins
Mop T.W. Stewart
Furniture Caster David A. Fisher
Stairclimbing Wheelchair Rufus J. Weaver
Guitar Robert Flemming ,Jr
Helicopter Paul E. Williams
Golf Tee George F. Grant
Fire Escape Ladder J.B. Winters
Motor J. Gregory
Telephone Transmitter Granville T. Woods
Lantern Micheal Harney
Electric Cutoff Switch Granville T. Woods
Thermo Hair Curlers Soloman Harper
Relay Instrument Granville T. Woods
Gas Burner B.F. Jackson
Telephone System Granville T. Woods
Kitchen Table H.A. Jackson
Galvanic Battery Granville T. Woods
Video Commander Joseph N. Jackson
Electric Raillway System Granville T. Woods
Remote Controllers Joseph N. Jackson
Roller Coaster Granville T. Woods
Sani-Phone Jerry Johnson
Auto Air Brake Granville T. Woods

Biscuit Cutter   A.P. Ashbourne
Super Soaker   Lonnie Johnson
Folding Bed   L.C. Bailey
Bicycle Frame Issac R. Johnson
Coin Changer   James A. Bauer
Space Shuttle Retrieval Arm   Wm. Harwell
Rotary Engine Andrew J. Beard
Printing Press W.A. Lavallette
Car Couple Andrew J. Beard
Envelope Seal F.W. Leslie
Letter Box   G.E. Becket
Laser Fuels   Lester Lee
Stainless Steel Pads   Alfred Benjamin
Pressure Cooker Maurice W. Lee
Torpedo Discharger H. Bradberry
Window Cleaner A.L. Lewis
Disposable Syringe Phil Brooks
Pencil Sharpener John L. Love
Home Security System Marie Brown
Fire Extinguisher Tom J. Marshal
Corn Planter Henry Blair
Lock   W.A. Martin

Information and chart By Paul Rider

CHAPTER 17

A TRIBUTE

This book is dedicated to African ancestors throughout the diaspora, honoring those we have lost to lynching and injustice.

For centuries, African people have been stripped of their culture, their land, their names, their spirituality, and their very lives—all in the name of colonization and oppression. This injustice did not begin with the transatlantic slave trade; it reaches back even further to the deliberate dismantling of great African civilizations. Our ancestors, the architects of dynasties, the visionaries behind towering pyramids, and the keepers of profound knowledge had their identities stolen and their stories rewritten.

Across the world, Black people have endured the unthinkable: ripped from their homeland, enslaved, lynched, and subjected to relentless attempts to erase our truth. Yet, despite every effort to break us, we rose. Like a phoenix emerging from the fire, we reclaimed our power, voices, and historical places. We are not simply survivors; we are the builders of nations, the pioneers of mathematics, astronomy, and architecture, the innovators in farming, Architecture, and science, and the heartbeat of civilization itself.

Through the depths of unimaginable pain, we have persevered. We have turned sorrow into strength, oppression into resilience, and injustice into a legacy of unyielding triumph.

This dedication stands as a testament to those we have lost and a vow never to let their stories be forgotten. Our ancestors' blood runs through our veins, and their fight lives on in us.

We are still here. We are still rising. And we will never be erased.

REFERENCES

1. "Art History." (n.d.). Interesting Africa Facts.

2. "African Art History 2010-2020." (n.d.). Contemporary African Art.

3. "African Mathematics." (n.d.). Taneter.

4. "Artist Ellis Wilson." (n.d.). Invaluable.

5. Bataine, M. (n.d.). "Mali Ancient Manuscripts: Showcasing the Civilization of West Africans During the Middle Ages." Heritage Daily.

6. Baxter, J. (2000, December 13). "Africa's 'Greatest Explorer'." BBC News.

7. Belyh, A. (2018, February 20). "How Jay-Z Started His Entrepreneurial Projects." Cleverism.

8. "BHA African American Athletes." (n.d.). My Black History.

9. "Biography of Professor James Small and Leonard Jeffries." (n.d.). Sankofa Speaks.

10. "Black Culture Connection." (n.d.).

11. Blanco, L. (2019, July 22). "The Secret to Master P's Millionaire Mindset and Business Success." Black Enterprise.

12. Brewer, D. L. (n.d.). "Grace Bumbry Biography."

13. Cartwright, M. (2019, February 22). "Timbuktu." World History Encyclopedia.

14. Chamberlain, G. (2015, January 24). "Philip Emeagwali." Black Inventor.

15. Collazo, J. S. (2017, January 4). "NASA's Hidden Figures: The Unsung Women You Need to Know." Biography.

16. Contributor, A. (2013, October 7). "When Black Men Ruled the World: 8 Contributions the Moors Made to Europe." Atlanta Black Star.

17. Craven, J. (2019, May 22). "The Famous Black Architects in U.S. History." ThoughtCo.

18. Craven, J. (2019, November 10). "Black Architects After the Civil War." ThoughtCo.

19. Dahlgren, K., & Arkin, D. (2017, June 28). "Inventor Bishop Curry." NBC News.

20. "Denmark Vesey." (2014, April 2). Biography.

21. "Dr. Llaila Afrika." (2020, March 22).

22. "Dr. Runoko Rashidi." (n.d.).

23. "Dr. Sebi Biography." (n.d.). Usha Village.

24. "Dr. Umar Johnson." (n.d.).

25. REMOE. (2018). "A Brief History of Reggae Music: From Jamaica to the World." The Palms Jamaica.

26. Morelle, R. (2014, January 27). "Science Reporter." BBC World Service.

Most of the information in this book can also be found on:
- BlackHistory.com
- Britannica.com
- BlackHistory.net
- Biography.com

- WorldHistory.com
- History.com

Some photos in this book were created using AI tools like Canva, Craiyon AI, and Pixabay powered by iStock.

A message from the Author

I have come to understand that the world would be dull and flavorless without the contributions of Black people. The African diaspora has profoundly enriched global culture.

Black Africans are the original inhabitants of our planet, the first ancestors who walked upright and established early civilizations.

We are the builders of civilizations, inventors, innovators, farmers, creators, and trendsetters. When you acknowledge your greatness, you are destined for success, and knowledge is an asset that can never be taken from you. It's essential to recognize that Black history is world history.

Embrace your greatness and ensure that you pass this knowledge on to your children.

KNOW YOUR GREATNESS!

-ELOGEIA HADLEY

"A people without the knowledge of their past
history,
origin, and culture is like a tree without roots."
~ Marcus Garvey

www.ingramcontent.com/pod-product-compliance
Lightning Source LLC
Chambersburg PA
CBHW050441150626

46551CB00028B/791

9798992580501